AF598891

GROUND

M10 Gun Motor Carriage

and the 17-Pounder Achilles Tank Destroyer

DAVID DOYLE

Library of Congress Control Number: 2022932058

Cover design by Justin Watkinson
Type set in Impact/Minion Pro/Univers LT Std

ISBN: 978-0-7643-6486-0
Printed in China

Published by Schiffer Publishing, Ltd.
4880 Lower Valley Road
Atglen, PA 19310
Phone: (610) 593-1777; Fax: (610) 593-2002
Email: Info@schifferbooks.com
Web: www.schifferbooks.com

Acknowledgments

This book would not have been possible without a great deal of help from my friends, including Tom Kailbourn, Jim Gilmore, Scott Taylor, Rob Ervin, Marc Sehring, Paul Bird, John Blackman, the late Don Moriarty, and the staff at the National Archives, Patton Museum, Ordnance Museum, and US Army Engineer School History Office. Of course, this book would not have been possible at all without the help and encouragement of my wife, Denise, who is my best friend and a true blessing.

Contents

Introduction

During the war, the American strategy concerning combating tanks was summarized by the historical officer of the Tank Destroyer Center as such: "Antitank doctrine of the United States Army at the time of the fall of France ran contrary to our historical military policy in that it implied passive defense rather than offensive action. Current field manuals stressed the importance of antitank mines and guns, but so far as their employment was taught, they were purely defensive weapons. Only the armored divisions thought in terms of aggressive methods against tanks." This final statement further hints at another detail of the planning of the day—each arm of the Army was responsible for its own antitank defense.

Gradually, the War Department began to move toward a strategy built on the aggressive use of mobile antitank units employing "stealthy reconnaissance and destroy[ing] the enemy armored elements by gun fire from carefully chosen locations."

While retrospectively, another tank seems an obvious solution, the strategists of the day preferred an antitank weapon that was faster and better armed than tanks of the time—and, not insignificantly, less expensive than a tank.

In fact, this last item was clear in Gen. Leslie McNair's remarks that "certainly it is poor economy to use a $35,000 medium tank to destroy another tank when the job can be done by a gun costing a fraction as much. Thus the friendly armored force is freed to attack a more proper target, the opposing force as a whole, in much the same manner as seacoast defenses free the Navy for offensive action at sea."

From this mindset in late 1941, the concept of a separate tank destroyer force began to jell. This force would be armed with specialized weapons. While the army's primary antitank weapon of the late 1930s was 37 mm towed antitank guns, these were soon deemed to be inadequate against enemy armor. Accordingly, the quest for larger weapons began, as did the desire for a self-propelled antitank gun—or gun motor carriage (GMC). The initial efforts involved adapting ¾-ton Dodge trucks to mount antitank weapons (the M6, née WC-55), which were intended as interim and training vehicles pending development of the M8 armored car for use by the tank destroyer reconnaissance force. In the same manner, half-tracks were fitted with cannon, yielding the interim M3 75 mm Gun Motor Carriage. But the quest was on to create a specialized and ideal tank destroyer, utilizing a tank chassis as the basis.

Two unsuccessful attempts were made to mount the 3-inch gun in a modified hull of an M3 medium tank. By January 1942, a prototype was in the works to mount the weapon in an open-top turret on the chassis of the twin GM diesel-powered M4A2 Sherman medium tank. After some months of development, a design was created at Aberdeen Proving Ground for a vehicle sharing the suspension, lower hull, and engine with the M4A2 but with an upper hull made from thinner armor plate. It was hoped that the weight savings would produce increased automotive performance. This vehicle was designated the T35.

Developed in the summer of 1941, the Dodge WC-55, also known by the military designation M6, combined a 37 mm antitank gun with the agile ¾-ton Dodge truck chassis to create a tank destroyer. Unfortunately, combat experience showed that the 37 mm lacked the power to defeat much of the German armor encountered. Accordingly, many of the vehicles were converted to ¾-ton weapons carriers (trucks), some even before having the weapons mounted. In the Pacific the M6 proved more successful, however, and had a longer service life in that theater. *National Archives via Jim Gilmore*

Surprised by the savage effectiveness of German armor in the 1939–1940 Blitzkrieg, in June 1941 the US Army Ordnance Department ordered an expedient self-propelled antitank gun built. It consisted of a 75 mm gun M1897A4 on an M2A3 carriage, installed facing forward at the front of the crew compartment of a half-track personnel carrier M3. A pilot vehicle was quickly designed and constructed at Aberdeen Proving Ground and was designated the 75 mm Gun Motor Carriage T12. When the vehicle showed promise, the army contracted with the Autocar Co. for eighty-six additional examples. *Patton Museum*

In late 1941, design work began on the 3-inch GMC T35, a tank-destroyer pilot based on the M4A2 medium tank. Fisher Tank Division completed the T35 by April 1942, and the vehicle is seen during trials at Aberdeen Proving Ground on April 23, 1942. *National Archives*

In a view of the T35 from the left rear, lifting eyes are visible on the rear and the upper front of the turret. Inside the turret is the lower part of the left periscope, fitted with a curved eye guard. The vertical-volute bogie brackets had the return roller at the top. *National Archives*

While work on the T35 pilot was proceeding, the T35E1, also built by the Fisher Tank Division, was produced. It featured a turret similar to that of the T35 but mounted on a specially constructed, lower-silhouette hull that capitalized on thin, sloped armor. Very faintly visible on the side of the hull of the T35E1 is its US Army (USA) registration number, W-4027648; the USA number of the T35 was W-4027647. The upper hull of the T35E1 would serve as the pattern for that of the 3-inch GMC M10. *National Archives*

Like the turret of the T35, that of the T35E1 had a pronounced bulge with a hard, straight edge around the circumference, and a partially open top, with a fixed periscope and a rotating periscope on the roof plate. The driver's hatch was hinged on the outboard side. *National Archives*

CHAPTER 1

The M10/M10A1

The T35E1 was standardized as the 3-inch GMC M10 in June 1942. This M10, USA registration number 4041014, as photographed at the Ordnance Operation, General Motors Proving Ground, on July 8, 1943, had a hull of mild steel, and to signify this, "SOFT PLATE MODEL" was lettered on the hull by welding. *Joe DeMarco collection*

Following an assessment of the fighting conditions in the Philippines, the Tank Destroyer Board requested that any new tank destroyers have a lower silhouette. The vehicle utilizing the M4A2 chassis with sloping-armor upper hull was redesigned accordingly by Aberdeen, with the new concept initially designated the 3-inch Gun Motor Carriage T35E1. It utilized the open-top turret of the T35, with a new hull featuring a lower profile and sloping armor.

A contract was awarded to the Fisher Tank Division of General Motors, which began detailed design work in January 1942. By April, Fisher had completed pilots of the T35 as well as the T35E1. Both pilots were equipped with cast open-top turrets, but subsequent testing indicated that a turret made of rolled armor plate would offer better protection.

On June 4, 1942, Ordnance Committee action 18313 recommended the standardization of the T35E1 as the 3-inch Gun Motor Carriage M10.

Production of the M10 began at the Fisher Grand Blanc Tank Arsenal in September 1942. The production vehicles differed from the prototype in several details, one of which was the gun mount. The mount was simplified and featured removable trunnion pins. The intent of this design feature was that this would allow the 3-inch gun to be exchanged for a 105 mm howitzer, or notably a British 17-pounder gun.

The urgent need for tank destroyers led the Army to issue a contract to Ford Motor Company for a similar vehicle, albeit powered by the Ford GAA gasoline engine. Ford began production of this vehicle, which was designated M10A1, in October 1942. Visually, larger louvered doors over the engine compartment distinguished the M10A1 from the M10. This vehicle remained in production at Ford until September 1943, when Ford was taken out of the tank and tank destroyer business by the government. Ford had produced 1,038 M10A1s up to that point.

Three different versions of turrets were mounted on the M10-series vehicles. Originally, the turret had no counterweights on the rear, but due to the imbalance caused by the gun, it was difficult to rotate the turret when on a grade. Field units improvised various types of counterweights in an attempt to overcome this deficiency. Eventually, new vehicles were factory-equipped with two 1,800-pound counterweights attached to the turret rear to correct this. In March 1943, the turret was redesigned, with the angle of the rear wall being changed and an enlarged counterweight added. The new turret was introduced into production in June. The next month the raised bosses on the hull and turret sides, intended for mounting supplemental armor (which was never produced), were eliminated.

M10A1 production was shifted to Grand Blanc, where they were produced along with the GM diesel-powered M10. Production of the M10 ceased in December 1943, by which time Fisher had built 4,993. Fisher production of complete M10A1 Gun Motor Carriages had stopped in November 1943, with a total of 375 being built. However, in January 1944, an additional 300 M10A1 chassis were completed for utilization in the production of 90 mm Gun Motor Carriage M36. These 300 chassis were counted in M10A1 production, raising the total to 675.

The M10A1s were used in the United States for training purposes, while, counter to the normal US Army policy against diesel-powered vehicles, troops overseas were issued the M10.

Also shipped overseas were 443 3-inch gun motor carriages supplied to the Free French, fifty-two to the Soviet Union, and

Pilot 3-inch GMC M10, USA number W-4040705, is undergoing analysis at Aberdeen Proving Ground on September 9, 1943. Bosses with nuts and washers on the upper hull and turret were for installing appliqué armor, but this armor was not used in practice. *National Archives*

1,648 to the British Empire. The British designated their early production vehicles the 3-inch Self-Propelled Mount Mk. I, and the later vehicles, with the extended "duckbill" counterweights, as 3-inch Self-Propelled Mount Mk. II.

While at the time they were fielded, many felt that the M10 and M10A1 were the best self-propelled antitank weapons on the battlefield, they failed to impress Gen. Andrew D. Bruce, the first head of the Tank Destroyer force. The M10 was standardized despite his objections; however, he continued to view the vehicle, like the M3 Gun Motor Carriage, as an interim vehicle.

While US antitank doctrine ultimately changed, rendering all the tank destroyers obsolete after World War II, many of these vehicles were supplied to other nations, and in fact some survived as combat vehicles into the twenty-first century.

Because the M10 turret lacked much of a rear overhang, the weight of the gun made it difficult to traverse it under certain conditions. To counteract this, early in the M10's service, racks of track grousers were placed on the rear of the turret for counterweights. *National Archives*

Workers at Fisher Body Division's Grand Blanc Arsenal in Michigan assemble M10s. The upper hulls and turrets were fabricated on the lower hull and chassis of the M4A2 medium tank. The main armament was the 3-inch gun M3 on the Mount M5. *Library of Congress*

Ford Highland Park assembly line workers go about their tasks, with M10A1s on the left line and M4A3 medium tanks to the right. These turrets are equipped with wedge-shaped counterweights, which superseded the slab-shaped "quick fix" counterweights. Designed by Fisher Tank Arsenal, these counterweights were assigned part numbers E7992 (right) and E7993 (left) and weighed a combined 3,700 pounds. On the floor between the two assembly lines is a roll of tracks and, farther away, several M10A1 turret assemblies.

A General Motors 6046 diesel engine, the power plant for the M10, is viewed from the left front. The 6046 engine was composed of two GM 6-71 diesel engines, which fed their output via flywheels to a double-clutch housing and a power transfer unit, which then transferred output to the driveshaft, often called the propeller shaft. The diesel power plant was preferred in part due to the lower flash point of that fuel as compared to gasoline.

Powering the M10A1 was the Ford GAA V-8, four-cycle, liquid-cooled engine, the same engine used in the M4A3 Sherman. The GAA used gasoline, had a displacement of 1,100 cubic inches, and developed a maximum net horsepower of 450 at 2,600 rpm and 500 maximum gross horsepower at 2,600 rpm. A Ford GAA is viewed from the rear end, as it was installed in the vehicle. On the top are the two Bendix Stromberg NA-45G carburetors and their manifold, to the sides of which are the camshaft housings. In the foreground are the two four-cylinder magnetos. On the side is the left exhaust manifold. *Patton Museum*

General Data

Model	**M10**	**M10A1**
Weight (combat)	65,200 lbs.	64,000 lbs.
Length*	286.3	286.3
Width*	120	120
Height*	114	114
Track	83 in.	83 in.
Crew	5	5
Maximum speed	25 mph	26 mph
Fuel capacity	165 gallons	168 gallons
Range	200 miles	115 miles
Electrical	24 negative ground	24 negative ground
Transmission speeds	5	5
Turning radius	31 feet	31 feet
Armament		
main	3-inch gun M7	3-inch gun M7
flexible	1× .50 M2 HB	1× .50 M2 HB

Overall dimensions listed in inches. Measure with main gun facing forward, and antiaircraft machine gun mounted.

Engine Data M10	
Engine make/model*	GMC 6046 or 6046D diesel
Number of cylinders	12
Cubic inch displacement	850
Horsepower	375 @ 2,100
Torque	855 @ 1,300
Governed speed (rpm)	2,100

Engine Data M10A1	
Engine make/model*	Ford GAA
Number of cylinders	60-degree V-8
Cubic inch displacement	1,100
Horsepower	450 @ 2,600
Torque	950 @ 2,100
Governed speed (rpm)	2,600

Radio Equipment
The M10 was equipped with SCR 610 radio set, RC99 interphone, and a M238 flag set.

Registration Numbers				
Model	**Quantity**	**Contract Number**	**Registration Number**	**Serial #**
M10	1,800	374-ORD-1880	4040705 thru 4042504	3 thru 1802
M10	1,200	374-ORD-1880	4081054 thru 4082253	2839 thru 4038
M10	1,117	374-ORD-1880	40110110 thru 40111226	5991 thru 7107
M10A1	1,038	374-ORD-1213	4046509 thru 4047546*	1803 thru 2840
M10A1	375	374-ORD-1213	40112380 thru 40112754	7984 thru 8358

* 200 registration numbers canceled

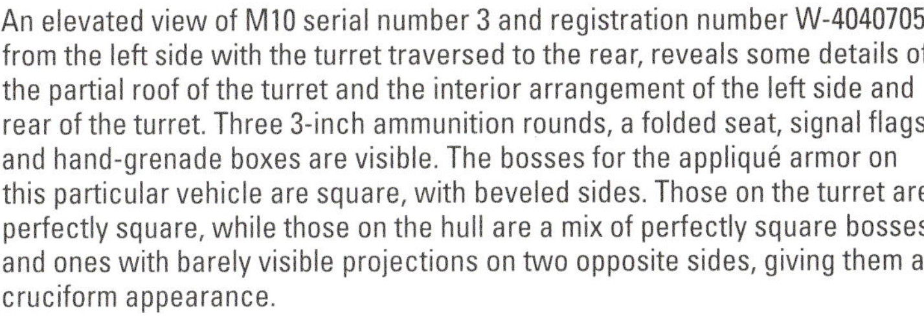
An elevated view of M10 serial number 3 and registration number W-4040705, from the left side with the turret traversed to the rear, reveals some details of the partial roof of the turret and the interior arrangement of the left side and rear of the turret. Three 3-inch ammunition rounds, a folded seat, signal flags, and hand-grenade boxes are visible. The bosses for the appliqué armor on this particular vehicle are square, with beveled sides. Those on the turret are perfectly square, while those on the hull are a mix of perfectly square bosses and ones with barely visible projections on two opposite sides, giving them a cruciform appearance.

In October 1942, Ford Motor Company began rolling out the gasoline-powered version of the M10, the 3-inch GMC M10A1. Fisher took over production of these vehicles in September 1943. As seen in an elevated photo of M10A1 serial number 1804 and registration number W-4046510, the ventilation grille doors on the engine deck were larger than on the M10, and the arrangement of the armored filler caps was different. The three rods on the roof of the turret and the one on the right rear of the turret were supports for a canvas cover for the turret; they swiveled down, as shown, when not in use.

The M10A1 was introduced in order to increase production of tank destroyers, It was virtually identical to the M10 but had a Ford gasoline engine instead of the General Motors 6046 diesel engine of the M10. The round bosses along the hull were mounting points for the proposed appliqué armor. *Patton Museum*

Although the M10 and the M10A1 were nearly indistinguishable from most angles, this left-rear view of an M10A1 shows one difference: the exhaust deflector below the rear overhang of the hull. The M10A1 also had a wider grille on the rear deck than the M10. A simple travel lock (called "gun rest" in the technical manuals) for the 3-inch gun M7 tube was on the center rear of the engine deck. *Patton Museum*

Early-production M10, USA number 4041128, nicknamed "Deadeye," was photographed at Armored Force Headquarters, Fort Knox, in 1943. "M-10" was marked on the turret, and the nickname was above an earlier, rubbed-out version of nickname. *Patton Museum*

"Deadeye" is viewed from the front at Fort Knox, showing the one-piece, cast final-drive assembly, T51 rubber-block tracks, the siren mounted on the left of the bow, and other features. Casting marks are visible on the upper part of the final-drive assembly. *Patton Museum*

"Deadeye" is observed from the left, showing the grouser racks, without grousers, mounted on the upper rear of the turret. Early on, these were conceived as a counterbalance for the front-heavy gun and turret, but they proved ineffective. *Patton Museum*

As viewed from above, the engine deck arrangement of 1942 production, Fisher-manufactured "Deadeye" is apparent, as is the Browning M2 .50-caliber machine gun on a pintle mount at the rear of the turret. Swivel-mounted rods, three on the top front of the turret and four at the rear, were designed to support a canvas top. *Patton Museum*

After the grousers attached to the rears of the early M10 turrets failed to provide sufficient counterbalance effect, wedge-shaped counterweights, *left*, were developed. Later, a scooped counterweight dubbed the duckbill was installed on M10 turrets, as seen on the vehicle to the right. *CECOM History Office*

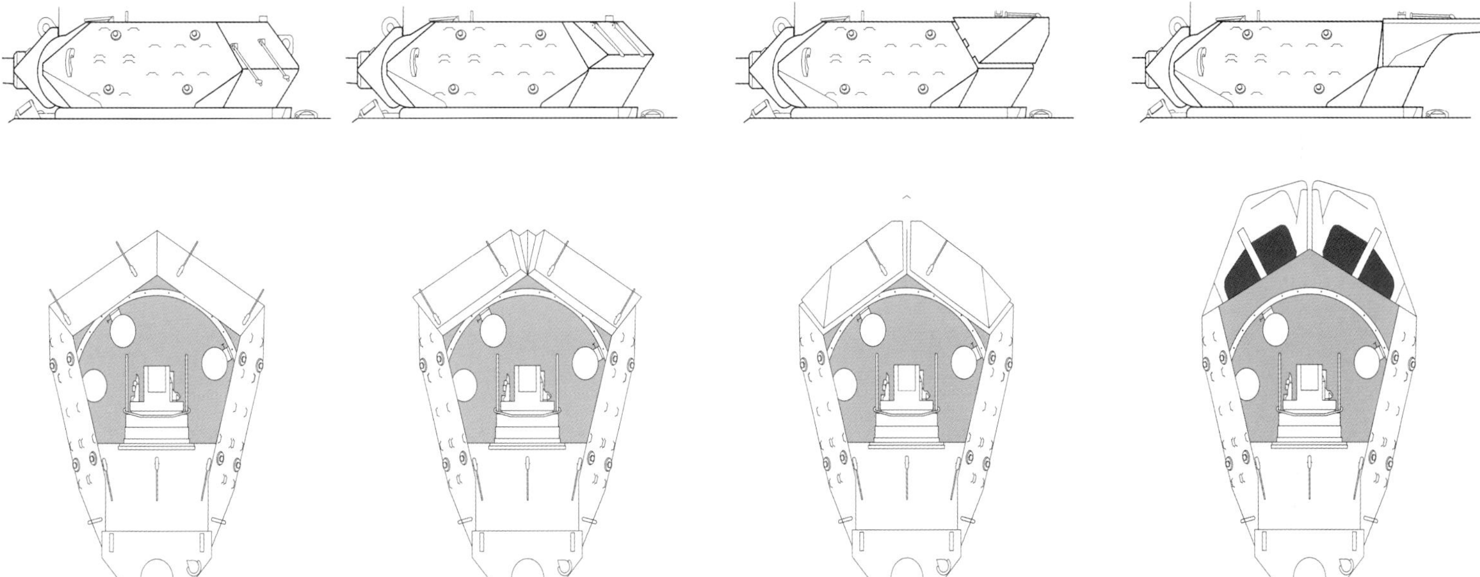

The original turret of the M10, *left*, had little weight in the rear to counterbalance the mass of the gun barrel projecting from the front of the turret. The early-production turret had box-shaped counterweights added to the rear. Mid-production turrets employed wedge-shaped counterweights, while late-production M10 turrets featured the scooped "duckbill" counterweights.

M10 registration number 4081950 is observed from the right rear with turret traversed to the rear, 3-inch gun tube resting in the travel lock, and a measuring stick propped up against the rear of the hull. Under the rear overhang of the upper hull is an exhaust deflector, with closed sides and a reinforced rear edge. A grouser-storage rack is on the sponson, and bosses, washers, and bolts are still present on the sponson and turret; later, these would be deleted from the sponsons.

In a shop, an M10 turret has been hoisted from the hull; the rear lifting eye is between the weights. A cutout was designed into the top front of each counterweight to give clearance to a swiveling support rod for a canvas top. Other rods are at the rear corners of the turret and on top of the turret roof. The 3-inch gun is secured to a travel lock attached to the lower surface of the turret roof.

The National Museum of Americans in Wartime preserves this mid-production example of an 3-inch GMC M10. A step is welded to the final-drive assembly, or differential cover, and a grab handle is attached to the glacis by two of the bolts originally intended as part of the attachments for appliqué armor. Also on the glacis are service headlights with blackout marker lamps on top, brush guards, and, on the left side, a siren. *Marc Sehring*

The counterweights on the rear of the turret are the mid-production wedge-shaped articles. Black-painted grousers are mounted on the rack on the sponson. Two webbing straps are attached to footman loops on the turret. *Marc Sehring*

The turret is traversed to the left, showing the angular design of the mantlet (referred to as "gun shield" in the M10 technical manuals). On the left-hand side of the mantlet is the teardrop-shaped cover for the aperture for the gunner's sight. *Marc Sehring*

Solid-disk bogie wheels are present on the M10. In the indentation on the forward part of the sponson, a base unit for a radio antenna is installed. Cutouts incorporated into the turret counterweight are evident. *Marc Sehring*

Welded to the inner sides of the brush guards are cylindrical holders for plugs, which were inserted in the headlight-mounting sockets when those lights were not installed. Casting marks are prominent on the upper part of the final-drive assembly. The driver's two periscopes are in the raised position, while those of the assistant driver are closed. *Marc Sehring*

The driver's hatch door is open, showing the periscope, in a holder on a rotating mount. The tracks are a smooth rubber-shoe type, likely the type T51. On the lower center part of the step is a brace, welded to the final-drive assembly. The cylindrical object welded to the glacis above the right headlight is a mount for a radio antenna. *Marc Sehring*

The Tank Museum at Saumur, France, preserves this 3-inch GMC M10, with the name "SIROCCO" painted on the sponson and markings for the Free French 2e Division Blindée (2nd Armored Division) on the vehicle. It is a mid-production vehicle, with bosses for attaching appliqué armor on the turret and sponsons, and wedge-shaped counterweights. The travel lock for the 3-inch gun consisted of a thin steel plate with a curved cutout on top; the cutout was lined with a strip of material, and some photos show rubber, sometimes peeling off, attached to it, to protect the paint on the gun barrel. *Pierre-Olivier Buan*

In a rear view of the M10 at Saumur, a tow pintle is visible below the slightly battered exhaust deflector. A tow cable is coiled on the engine deck. T48 tracks with well-worn rubber shoes with chevron grousers are installed. A gap is present between the two counterweights on the rear of the turret. *Pierre-Olivier Buan*

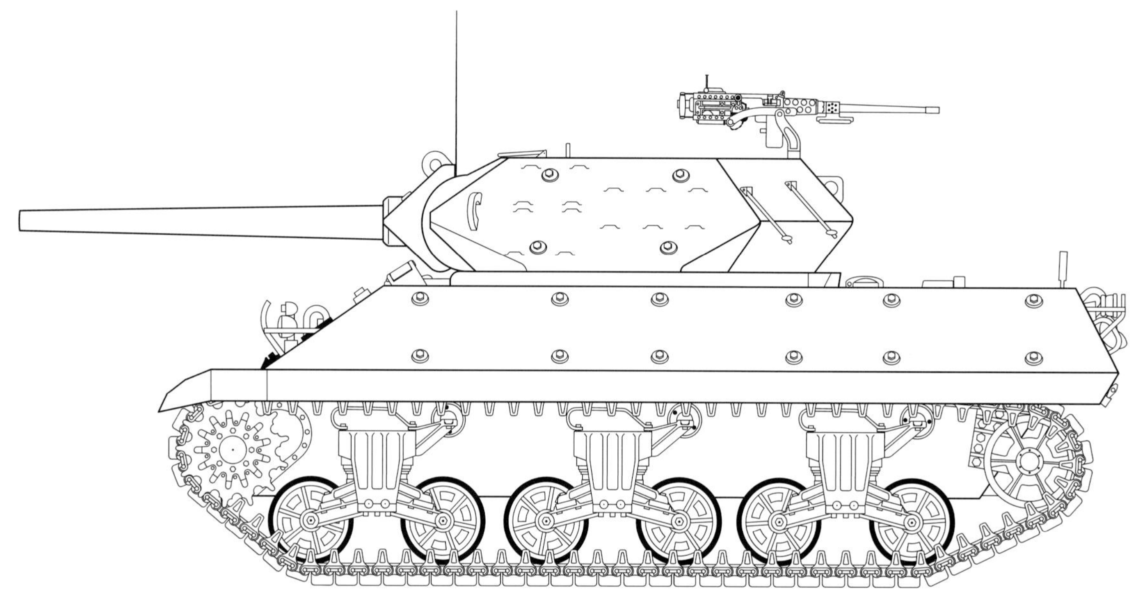

M10 GMC (early)

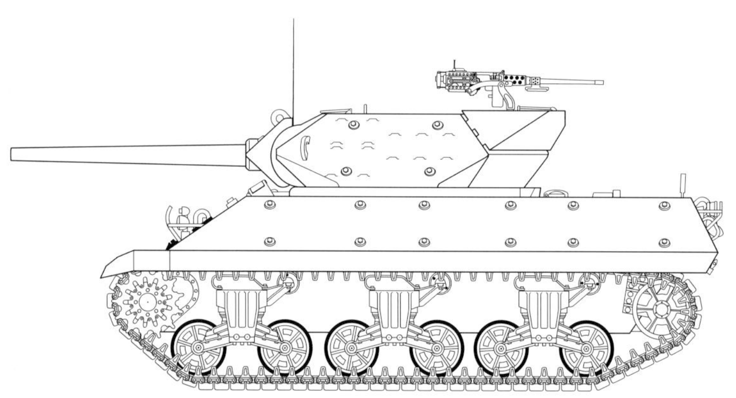

M10 GMC (mid-production)

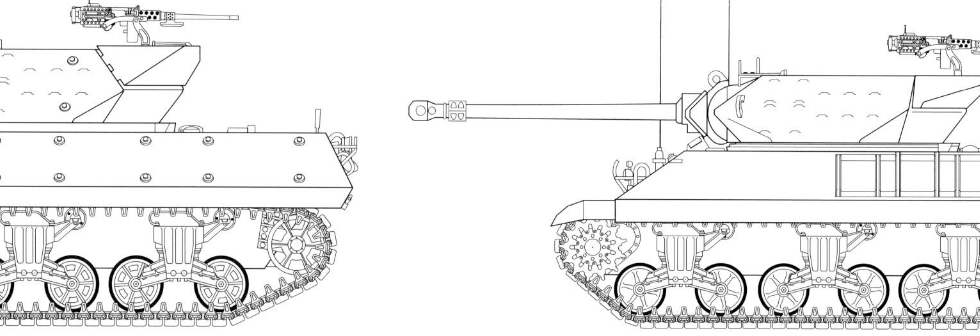

Achilles IIC

During the latter part of production of the 3-inch GMC M10, several changes were introduced, primary of which were the discontinuation of the bosses for mounting appliqué armor on the sponsons, and the introduction of redesigned counterweights, with a curved or scooped underside. These are sometimes referred to as "duckbill" counterweights On the mudguard above the sprocket of M10 registration number 40111053 (the third-from-last digit may be other than "0") is a stencil, "PREPARED BY L.T.D. 10/24/43."

On M10 registration number 401123901, which bears a "PREPARED BY L.T.D." stencil dated October 24, 1944, the four bosses for mounting appliqué armor on the side of the turret have been omitted. On the upper right corner of the glacis of this vehicle and the one in the preceding photo is a cylindrical bracket for a radio antenna.

Written in weld beads on the sponson of M10 serial number 632 and registration number 4041336, inside the grouser rack, is "SOFT PLATE MODEL." The vehicle was photographed during evaluations by the Ordnance Operation, General Motors Proving Ground, on August 18, 1943. Aside from the use of mild steel on the hull instead of armor plate, the vehicle resembles that of an early to mid-production M10, but the counterweights are the late production type. To the front of the grouser rack is a smaller rack that was associated with the 90 mm GMC M36; it was for storing a driver's windshield and hood assembly.

A late production M10 completed after July 1943 has been marked with the registration number 4041942, the nickname "HITLER'S NIGHTMARE," and replica markings for Company A, 601st Tank Destroyer Battalion. Bosses are present on the sides of the turret and on the glacis only. The counterweights remain the mid-production wedge-type articles. *David Doyle*

Steel strips are welded to the final-drive assembly and to the outer side of each of the front tow eyes, and, as a modification, a short piece of angle iron was welded to the upper right part of the final-drive assembly, likely as a handhold and step to assist the drivers in climbing up to their hatches. *Paul Bird*

In a view of the same M10 from the rear, an armored box for a telephone handset is below the right tow eye; this was for soldiers operating outside the tank to communicate with the crew. A metal conduit proceeds from the bottom of the box to under the hull next to the exhaust deflector. *Paul Bird*

Late-type, scooped counterweights on a 3-inch GMC M10 are observed from the lower left quarter. Casting marks are on the side of the counterweight near the turret and on the bottom, toward the right of the photo. *David Doyle*

The tops of the wedge counterweights of the M10 at Fort Hood are observed from inside the turret. Hex bolts and washers secure the weights to the upper-rear facets of the turret. On the lower right facet of the turret are racks for storing three ready rounds of 3-inch ammunition. Toward the bottom is the traversing ring gear.

The wedge-type counterweights of an M10 at the 3rd Cavalry Regiment Museum, at Fort Hood, Texas, are viewed from above and to the left rear. Clearances are incorporated into the counterweights for the rear lifting ring of the turret and the rods for supporting a canvas cover. Drain holes are on the tops of the counterweights; the right one is in view. Inside the turret adjacent to the rear lifting eye is the socket for an antiaircraft machine-gun cradle. The 3-inch gun breech is to the far left. *David Doyle*

Details of the mantlet and turret roof of the restored M10 nicknamed "HITLER'S NIGHTMARE" are seen from above the tube of the 3-inch gun. Casting marks are on the upper center of the mantlet, and a thick weld is on the joint between the mantlet and the sleeve for the 3-inch gun. A U-shaped splash guard on the right side of the mantlet mimics the splash guard for the aperture and teardrop-shaped cover for the gunner's sight aperture on the left side. *Don Moriarty*

The original travel lock for the breech end of the 3-inch gun, seen here as the small device with a chain attached, on the roof of the turret, was prone to failure, so a second travel lock was installed during production. It is the rod attached to the roof to the left of the original lock. Next to the seat toward the left is one of two traversing locks: turning it immobilized the traversing of the turret. Dual elevation handwheels were provided; the right one is on the side of the gun mount. On the side of the turret above the seat is a bracket for a portable fire extinguisher. *David Doyle*

As seen from the gunner's station in the left side of the turret of an M10, to the left is the traversing handwheel, to the right of which are the azimuth indicator (which shows the orientation of the turret with reference to the fore-and-aft centerline of the vehicle) and the left elevation handwheel. At the upper center is the mount for the gunner's telescopic sight, which typically was the M51 telescope. To the right is the gun cradle, which holds the 3-inch gun M7 between the two hydrospring-type recoil cylinders. *David Doyle*

In a view taken from the rear of the breech of the 3-inch gun, the yoke-shaped tube that extends from the sides of the gun to the upper front of the top of the breech is the manual firing handle. The vertical sliding breech is open, showing the plugged opening of the breech chamber. Also in view is the gunner's telescope to the front left of the gun, and the two travel locks above the gun. *Don Moriart*

In a view into the turret of an M10, the mannequin's right hand is above a bracket for mounting a panoramic sight, which was used in laying the gun in indirect-fire situations where the target was not in the line of sight. White-painted racks for ammunition are visible in the right sponson. Behind the mannequin's left elbow is the rack for a Thompson submachine gun and ammo clips for that weapon. To the lower right is the socket for the antiaircraft machine gun. *Don Moriarty*

A mannequin stands in the loader's station in the right rear of an M10 turret. Behind his upper arm is a rack for 440 rounds of .45-caliber ammunition in twenty-round magazines for a Thompson submachine gun. That gun was stored on the underside of the ammo rack. Also in view are the socket for the .50-caliber antiaircraft machine-gun cradle, and ready racks for 3-inch shells. *Don Moriarty*

Three members of the crew were posted in the turret of the M10, with the gunner located to the left of the gun. In a view of the right interior of the turret, the vehicle commander's round seat is to the left and the loader's is to the right. On the roof of the turret to the far left is a steel stiffener, which was welded on to reinforce the roof in order to be able to bear the load of the gun when the travel lock was engaged. *David Doyle*

In the same M10, a mannequin is standing in the gunner's station, hand on the traversing handwheel. The diamond-tread-plate floor of the fighting compartment had hinged panels, for access to storage compartments below, which, among other things, held the batteries and 300 rounds of .50-caliber ammunition. *Don Moriarty*

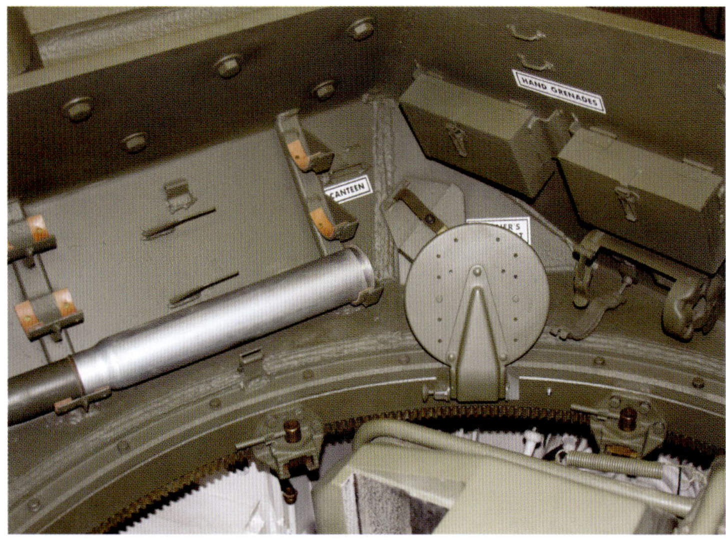

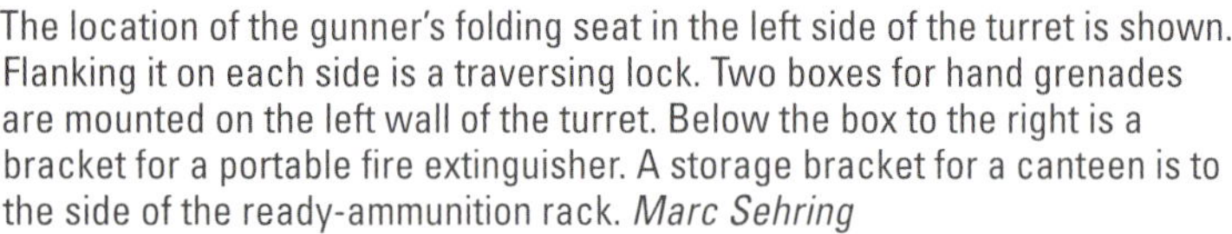
The location of the gunner's folding seat in the left side of the turret is shown. Flanking it on each side is a traversing lock. Two boxes for hand grenades are mounted on the left wall of the turret. Below the box to the right is a bracket for a portable fire extinguisher. A storage bracket for a canteen is to the side of the ready-ammunition rack. *Marc Sehring*

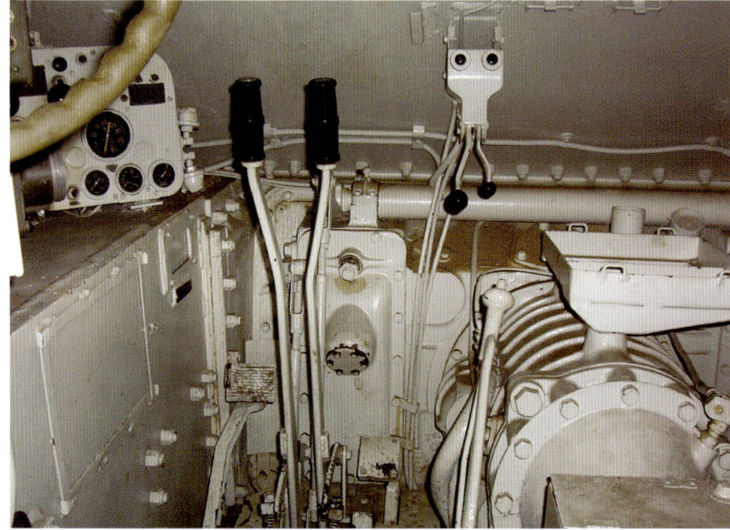

As seen from the driver's seat, to the left is the instrument panel, to the right of which are the steering-brake control levers, with the clutch pedal to the left of the bottoms of the steering-brake levers and the accelerator pedal to the right of the levers. The device mounted on the glacis to the upper right of center has two clutch-lockout buttons, with the throttle (*left*) and throttle lock lever (*right*) on the bottom of the box. In the font of the compartment is the left steering-brake housing and removable cover. To the lower right is the transmission, with the gearshift lever on its left side. *Don Moriarty*

The driver's compartment of an M10 is viewed from below the left side of the turret, with the left sponson racks for 3-inch ammunition to the left and the left elevating handwheel to the top. At the bottom is the driver's adjustable seat, and to the right of the spoke of the elevating handwheel is the driver's intercom box. *Don Moriarty*

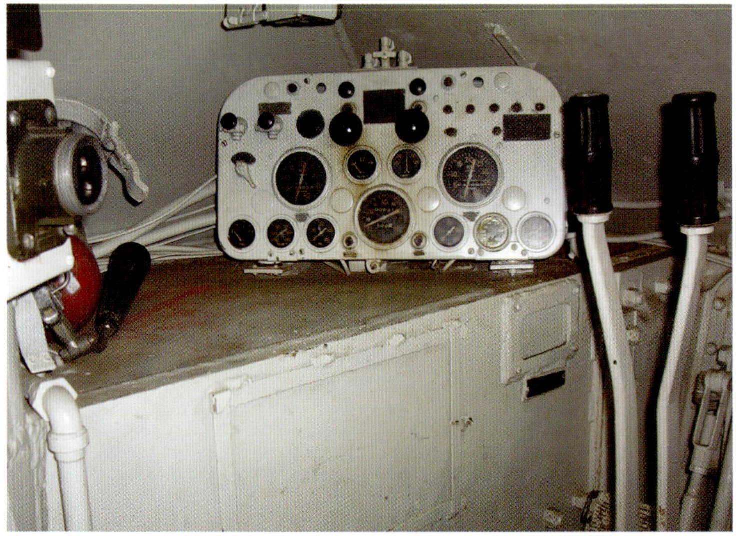

The instrument panel is located on the ledge in the front of the left sponson and is tilted for better visibility to the driver. It includes essential gauges, such as speedometer, tachometer, voltmeter, and ammeter, as well as a clock, light switches, circuit-breaker reset buttons, starter buttons, and other controls. *Don Moriarty*

CHAPTER 2

The 17-Pounder Achilles

After the British began receiving the 3-inch GMC M10 in 1943, Royal Ordnance factories replaced the 3-inch guns in many of them, substituting the very potent and reliable Ordnance QF 17-pounder antitank gun, mounting it in the existing turret. The resulting vehicle was assigned various official designations: M10C; 17-pounder M10 S.P. (self-propelled); Achilles IC; and 17-pounder, Self-propelled, Achilles. The vehicle was readily differentiated from the M10 by its main-gun barrel, which was longer than the 3-inch gun and was fitted with a distinctive, bulbous muzzle brake, to the immediate rear of which was a counterweight. The British reworked the gun shield and added other modifications.

US general Andrew Bruce was not alone in feeling that while the 3-inch weapon of the M10 was superior to that found on earlier US tank destroyers, it was inadequate against the ever-increasing weight of German armor. The British addressed this by rearming some of the nearly 1,700 M10s that they received with the superb 17-pounder quick-firing antitank cannon. The turret and gun mount of the M10 were specifically designed to facilitate this. The weapon used was a modification of the 17-pounder Mk. II, which was designated the 17-pounder Mk. V. From May 1944 through April 1945, beginning at the Royal Ordnance Factory in Woolwich, many of the M10s supplied to the British were rearmed with the more powerful guns. Ultimately, 1,017 of these vehicles were converted at Royal Ordnance Factories in Woolwich, Nottingham, Radcliffe, and Ellesmere Port. Vehicles so converted had a "C" suffix added to their model designation. The final conversions were made in April 1945.

A restored Achilles bears the nickname "GHENT" on the turret. Its turret is fitted with wedge-type counterweights. The gun shield differs in several respects from the one fitted on the M10. Also employed as the main gun of the Sherman Firefly, the 17-pounder was one of the most effective antitank weapons of World War II and outclassed the 3-inch gun M7 of the M10 regardless of the type of antitank ammunition used. *John Blackman*

A dome-shaped wireless antenna base is present on the cylindrical bracket adjacent to the right lifting ring on the glacis of "GHENT." A different type of antenna base with a short antenna is on the recessed mount in the sponson. Both of the racks on the sponson, for grousers and for two liquid containers, are attached by using bolts through appliqué-armor bosses. *John Blackman*

The dome-shaped wireless antenna base is visible above the right headlight brush guard. The sight aperture in the gun shield is basically a vertical slot. On some Achilles, the upper part of the slot was covered by an armored plate, leaving a small opening at the bottom. *John Blackman*

The canvas cover has been erected over the turret, supported by swiveling metal rods. Two racks, each with three spare track shoes, are welded to the final-drive assembly. The rearview mirrors are postwar additions. *John Blackman*

The bogie wheels on this Achilles are a mix of convex and concave solid-disk wheels and tamped-spoke wheels. The sprocket is the so-called "economy" model, part number D47366. The stamped-spoke idler is part number C85164. *John Blackman*

The canvas cover for the turret is viewed from the left front. A loop of rope is bound into the cover around the top and near the bottom. The bottom rope is exposed at the corners and center to allow the rope to be attached to hooks on the brackets for the front support rods. The same system is used on the rear of the cover. The tops of the support rods fit through grommets in the canvas. Straps secure the bottom of the cover to footman loops on the sides of the turret. *John Blackman*

An Achilles is viewed from the front with the driver's hatch open. On this vehicle, there are two cylindrical brackets for wireless antennas on the right side of the glacis: the standard one mounted above the headlight assembly, and an extra one to the right side of the right headlight. A grab handle is attached with washers and bolts to two of the bosses on the glacis, above the spare-track holders. *John Blackman*

The Achilles nicknamed "GHENT" is observed from the front. From this perspective, an enemy gunner would know that he was facing a 17-pounder or other powerful gun, if only from the presence of a muzzle brake. The ring on the front of the gun shield, through which the barrel of the gun passed, had a distinctive notch on the bottom. *John Blackman*

When the engine-compartment-door grilles were removed, inside the opening was an engine-compartment splash panel, a fairly thick reinforced steel shield designed to protect the engine and its accessories from bullet splash. The splash panel was hinged at the front (*toward the top of the photo*) and had a hold-open arm to immobilize it when maintenance was being performed on the engine. *John Blackman*

In a view down into the turret of an Achilles, the 17-pounder gun, cradle, recoil cylinders, recoil guard, and ejected-casing deflector occupy the center of the photo. On the rear of the turret are ready racks for six rounds of 17-pounder ammunition. Below the turret are more stored 17-pounder shells and the diamond-tread floor plates. At the bottom center is the travel lock for the gun. At the upper left is a rack for thirty-two magazines of 9 mm ammunition for Sten submachine guns. *John Blackman*

The engine-compartment splash shield has been secured in the raised position, revealing the top of the GM Detroit Diesel twin-diesel power unit. To each side are three oil-bath air cleaners. Above the front center of the engine are two engine-lubrication oil filters, to each side of which are a primary fuel oil filter and an air-heater coil box. *John Blackman*

On the right side of the breech of the 17-pounder gun is the breechblock-operating handle. Both types of travel lock are present and are attached to the turret roof. On the left side of the turret are, top to bottom, tank-distinguishing flags, two Sten guns, and a bracket for a portable fire extinguisher. *John Blackman*

Details of the recoil guard and the ejected-cartridge deflector are viewed from the right side of the turret. In each sponson (the left one is depicted at the center) were racks for twenty-two rounds of 17-pounder ammunition. In the Achilles, all fifty rounds of 17-pounder ammunition were stored in the turret and the sponsons, with none being stowed under the floor. Instead, a wide variety of equipment, tools, supplies, and accessories were stored under the floor. *John Blackman*

In the left front of the turret are the gunner's elevating handwheel (next to the gun cradle) and traversing handwheel. To the left of the left recoil cylinder is the telescopic gunsight. To the front of the fighting-compartment floor are the driver's seat and the transmission. *John Blackman*

At the top are, *left*, ready-ammunition racks and, *right*, stored Sten guns and a fire-extinguisher bracket on the right wall of the turret. Below the fire-extinguisher bracket is a turret traversing lock. Below the turret are stowed 17-pounder rounds in the left sponson. *John Blackman*

In the right rear of the turret of the Achilles, *looking to the left*, in the top half are ready rounds in their racks. Below the turret toward the left are two sections of a bore-cleaning staff, which the British referred to as "staves." To the lower right are 17-pounder cartridges in racks in the left sponson. *John Blackman*

The 17-pounder rounds are stored in alternating order, front to rear and vice versa, in the racks in the right sponson. On the hull below the sponson are five US crew canteens, hung from brackets. *John Blackman*

This is the view from below the turret of the Achilles to the driver's compartment. The green tube to the upper right is a cross-member spanning the bottom of the recoil guard. Above the driver's seat is the traversing handwheel. *John Blackman*

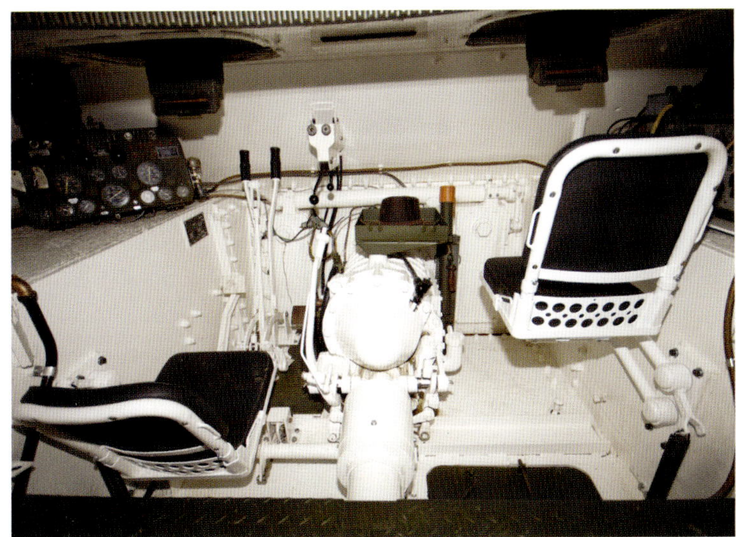

To the left are the instrument panel, driver's seat, and steering-brake levers. At the center is the transmission; the green tray on top of it was for storing periscopes and spare periscope heads. On the glacis above the transmission are the throttle controls and clutch lockout switches. To the right is the wireless operator's seat, showing the two swiveling arms and coil spring, attached to the hull, with which the seat could be raised and lowered. In the sponson is the wireless set. Toward the lower left, and partly hidden by the fighting-compartment floor, is the escape hatch. *John Blackman*

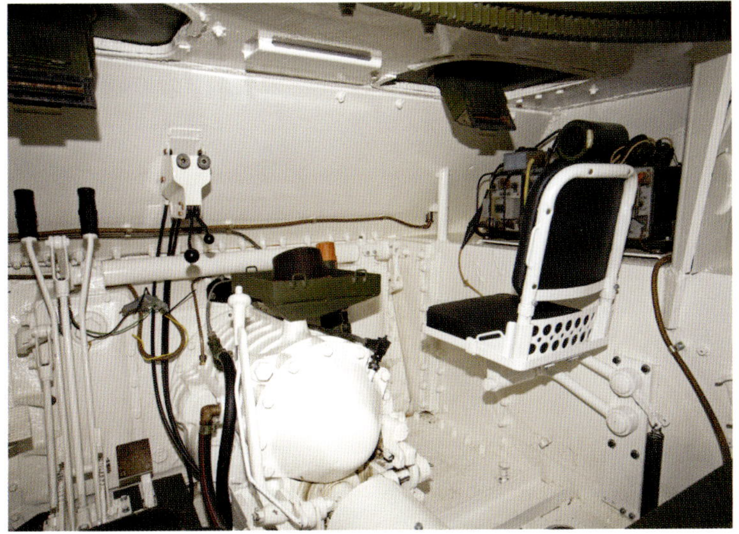

The transmission, wireless operator's seat, and wireless set are seen from a different perspective. Above the seat is the right hatch door, with a periscope on a rotating mount on it. At the bottom center is the front end of the cover for the propeller shaft. *John Blackman*

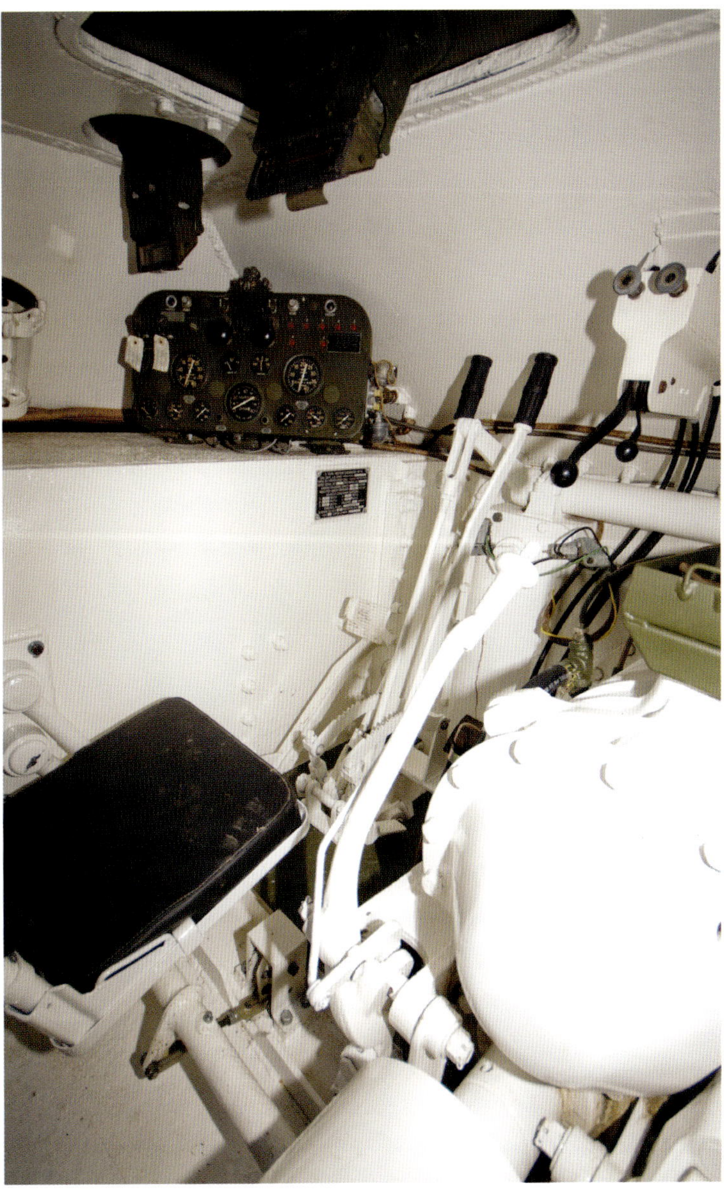

The driver's station is viewed from behind the transmission (*lower right*). On the left rear of the transmission is the shift lever. Screwed to the hull below the instrument panel is the data plate for this vehicle. The driver had two periscopes, both on rotating bases: one on the hatch door, and one to the left of the hatch door. *John Blackman*

CHAPTER 3

The M10/Achilles in Combat

To train crews and improve on doctrine and planning for the introduction of the M10 to combat in North Africa and beyond, the vehicle was tried out at the Desert Training Center in California, in 1943. This example has a trailer hitched to its tow pintle. *National Archives*

An M10 makes speed, stirring up a cloud of dust, during maneuvers at the Desert Training Center in 1943. Beyond the half-track to the right in the distance is another M10. Both vehicles have the wedge-shaped turret counterweights introduced in January 1943. *National Archives*

An M10 is in a dug-in position during training in 1943. Emplacing the tank destroyer in such a position in flat, open terrain offered protection to the crew and vehicle, but it was necessary to prepare the ditch in such way that the vehicle could quickly exit from it. *National Archives*

During Stateside training maneuvers in 1943, an M10 navigates a dusty trail. The turret is traversed to the rear, presenting the wedge-shaped counterweights, and a crewman is manning the .50-caliber machine gun. The vehicle is running on T49 steel tracks. *National Archives*

A dug-in M10 with wedge-shaped turret counterweights, possibly the same vehicle seen in the preceding photograph, has been further concealed by means of local camouflage: tree branches cut in the vicinity. A crewman is hands on at the .50-caliber machine gun. *National Archives*

An M10 and another to the left are parked during training exercises in the United States in 1943. The wheels are the open-spoke D38501, and the bogie assemblies are the B207881, with a horizontal casting seam below the top of each bogie bracket. *National Archives*

The same 3-inch GMC M10 shown in the preceding photo is viewed from the front. Welded on the right side of the final-drive assembly is an L-shaped plate that may have been intended as a foothold. Sewn to the front of the muzzle cover is a handle. *National Archives*

The M10 first saw combat in North Africa, with two tank destroyer battalions equipped with these vehicles, the 776th and 899th, entering the fray in Tunisia in March 1943. Shown here is one of the first M10s to arrive in theater, photographed on March 13, 1943. *National Archives*

On the left side of the hull of the same M10, the nickname "Invincible" is chalked inside a rectangular border; to the front of the hull is chalked a diamond with a "1" inside it. Splotches of what appear to be mud camouflage are on the hull, turret, and gun. *National Archives*

The same M10 was fitted with box-shaped turret counterweights; these ones were lead, as indicated by the retainer bands. Along with the grousers in the rack, three rubber track shoes are stowed on the rack. At the lower rear is a crumpled exhaust deflector. *National Archives*

Pioneer tools are in place on the rear of the M10, including a sledgehammer, crowbar, mattock head and handle, ax, and bogie wrench. The shovel is not installed on its holders. The number "311" is chalked below the right taillight assembly. *National Archives*

In a final photo of the M10 displayed in the preceding series, a chunk is missing from the sponson above the right sprocket. The front lifting eyes on the hull are the type that included a base plate. The lifting eye on the side of the turret had squared edges. *National Archives*

All five members of the crew of an M10 in Tunisia, including one with a Thompson submachine gun, pose for the photographer. A clear view is offered of the interiors of the driver's and assistant driver's hatch covers, with periscope holders and ring-type pulls. *University of Memphis*

An M10 crew of Company B. 811th Tank Destroyer Battalion, is engaged in a training exercise at Camp Carson, Colorado, on April 1, 1943. The number "1612" is painted in small numbers on the front of each fender; illegible writing is at the top of the glacis. *National Archives*

A Greek military attaché, Colonel Xanos, is taking a ride in the assistant driver's seat of an M10 assigned to the 811th Tank Destroyer Battalion at Camp Carson, Colorado, in April 1943. In the turret are a Capt. Parson (*left*), and Maj. Peter Clainos. *National Archives*

At Camp Carson, Colorado, in April 1943, an infantryman in the foxhole in the foreground has just thrown a practice grenade at an M10 that has just passed over him. The 3-inch gun is traversed to the rear and is lying in the stirrup-type travel lock. *National Archives*

An M10 tank destroyer is parked at the ordnance division of the Mediterranean Base Section at Oran, Algeria, on April 5, 1943. From this angle, it is difficult to see what type of turret counterweight was present; the following photo reveals it was the wedge type. *National Archives*

The M10 shown in the preceding photo is observed from the right rear. Standard vehicular items stowed on the sides of the turret included a 12-by-12-foot tarpaulin, camouflage netting, a canvas top, and five canvas musette bags for the crew. *National Archives*

This photo shows in close detail the damage done to the turret of an M10 tank destroyer by enemy gunfire during an engagement in North Africa in April 1943. There were several glancing hits, as well as a penetration at the top of the glacis, and the mantlet was gone. *National Archives*

In a study of an M10 crew at Camp Carson, Colorado, the commander is scanning for aerial threats while a crewman mans the .50-caliber machine gun and the gunner looks forward. On the glacis is an unusual rack with two rows of grousers. *National Archives*

A soldier is motioning the driver of an M10, apparently attempting to park it. A tarpaulin has been lashed over the turret: the appliqué armor bolts on the hull made handy fastening points. None of the pioneer tools are present on the rear of the vehicle. *National Archives*

An M10 is backing up to the ramp of *LST-346* at Pier 5, Newport News, Virginia, on April 22, 1943, for shipment overseas. The turret, featuring wedge counterweights, is traversed to the rear and covered with a tarpaulin. Headlight assemblies have been removed. *National Archives*

As viewed from inside *LST-346* at Newport News on April 22, 1943, an M10 is about to back down the ramp and into the ship. Pioneer tools on the rear plate of the hull have been removed, but both of the taillight assemblies are still mounted. Tracks are T51. *National Archives*

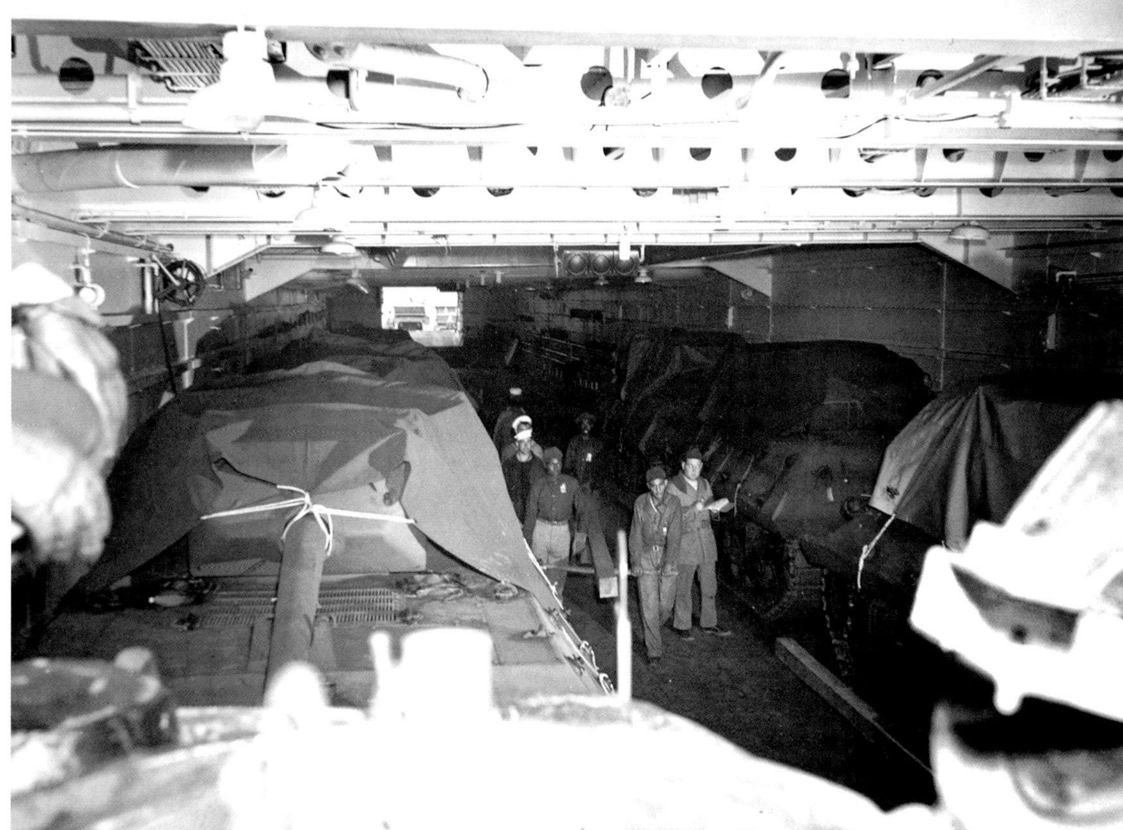

M10s are lined up on the second deck of *LST-346*, ready for shipment across the Atlantic. The men at the center are carrying large wooden beams, probably for chocking the vehicles so they didn't shift during transit. The front ramp is in the background. *National Archives*

During a military parade in Casablanca, French Morocco, on May 9, 1943, a group of M10s pass in review. According to original captioning of this photo, these were Lend-Lease vehicles, so they may have been operated by the Free French forces. *National Archives*

Members of the 631st Tank Destroyer Battalion are being instructed on the operation of the main weapon system in the M10 at Camp Shelby, Mississippi, on May 26, 1943. The US Army registration number, 4046634, is very faintly visible on the side of the hull. *National Archives*

SSgt. James T. Ivy of the 631st Tank Destroyer Battalion crawls out through the exit hatch in the bottom of the hull of an M10 at Camp Shelby, Mississippi, in June 1943. The hatch offered a means of exit if the vehicle rolled over or if it was under fire. *National Archives*

A column of M10s of Company A, 899th Tank Destroyer Battalion, are proceeding to Maknassy, Tunisia, on August 8, 1943. A very close inspection of the photograph reveals that under all the dust on the glacis of the lead vehicle is a white star. *National Archives*

An M10 crew of the 632nd Tank Destroyer Battalion is training in their turret on August 20, 1943. The crewman at the center is holding the breechblock crank. Each member was to be prepared to assume another's duties in the event of a casualty in battle. *Jim Gilmore collection*

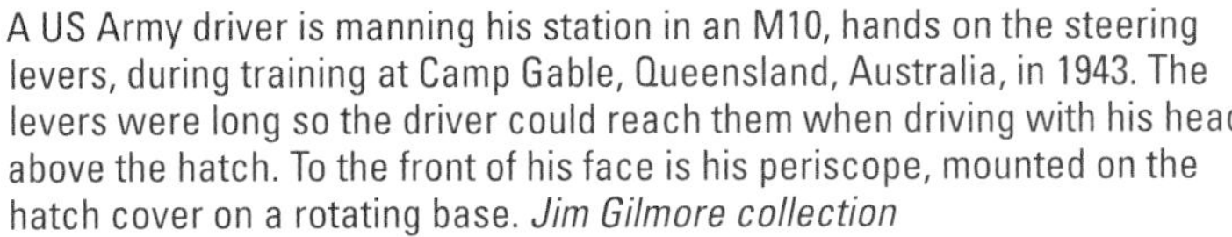

A US Army driver is manning his station in an M10, hands on the steering levers, during training at Camp Gable, Queensland, Australia, in 1943. The levers were long so the driver could reach them when driving with his head above the hatch. To the front of his face is his periscope, mounted on the hatch cover on a rotating base. *Jim Gilmore collection*

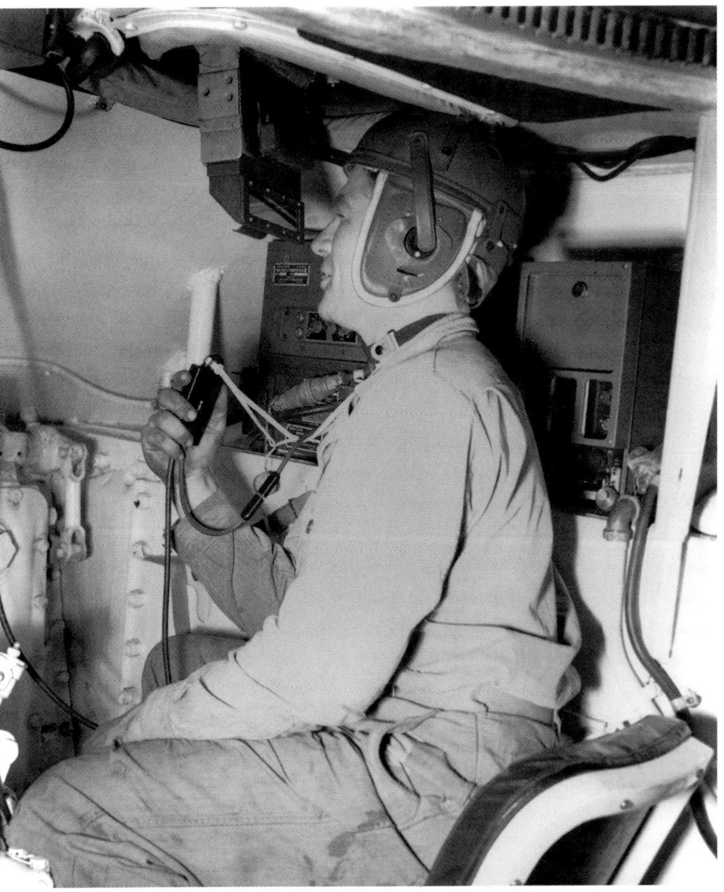

The assistant driver, to the right of the driver, was responsible for operating the radio to his right, relaying radio messages to and from the vehicle commander, observing to the front during firing, and taking over the driver's duties should the need arise. Here, an assistant driver looks through his periscope while holding his microphone switch. *Jim Gilmore collection*

An M10 tank destroyer crosses a pontoon bridge over the Volturno River in Italy on October 13, 1943. The gun motor carriage is approaching the photographer, and its turret is traversed to the rear. A white star with no circle is at the upper center of the glacis. *US Army Engineer School History Office*

In a posed photo, the crew of an M10 nicknamed "Pistol Packin' Mama" scans for aerial threats during a training exercise at Camp Hood, Texas, on October 16, 1943. The nickname was repeated on the final-drive assembly, along with the marking "TDS WD X-160." *Jim Gilmore collection*

As the war dragged on, it became common to use M10s for fire support, such as this dug-in number 3 gun of the 2nd Platoon, A Company, 701st Tank Destroyer Battalion, firing on enemy positions in the Mignano sector in Italy on December 12, 1943. *National Archives*

Three M10s, including the one in the foreground and two to the left, are parked, with turrets reversed and 3-inch guns in the travel locks, in woodland at an unspecified locale. Each vehicle has a tarpaulin over the open turret, supported by what appears to be a frame. *National Archives*

The Free French were users of the M10. Here, an M10 of the 7e Régiment de Chasseurs d'Afrique crosses a bridge in the Aquafondata area of Italy on January 20, 1944. What appears to be "CLEMENCEAU" is marked on the bow; logs are piled on the turret. *National Archives*

M10s saw service in the Pacific, and reportedly the first unit to take them into combat there was a tank battalion, as opposed to a tank destroyer battalion, the 767th, at Kwajalein. Here, an M10 of the 767th duels with a Japanese bunker on Kwajalein on February 4, 1944. *National Archives*

M10s of 98 Battery, Royal Canadian Artillery, are situated in a muddy field on February 27, 1944. British and Commonwealth forces designated their M10s the 3-inch Self-propelled Mount M10, or Wolverine. A red-white-red recognition flash is on the hull. *Imperial War Museum*

During a lull in the action on Kwajalein, several M10s stand by as their crews await their next assignments. The lead vehicle has suffered damage to its right fender and glacis. Grousers are fitted on the tracks at intervals for better traction on the island's sand. *National Archives*

In the Anzio area of Italy on February 29, 1944, an M10 of the 601st Tank Destroyer Battalion moves forward cautiously, on the lookout for German panzers that recently had effected a breakthrough. Ammunition packing tubes are piled on the rear deck. *National Archives*

Wiremen of the 15th Infantry Regiment repair communications wires ripped up by M10s of the 601st Tank Destroyer Battalion in the Anzio area on February 29, 1944. One of the offending M10s, parked in the background, has early, box-shaped turret counterweights. *National Archives*

In a posed photo, the French crew of an M10 have manned their vehicle and are awaiting photos to move out, in the Venafro area, Italy, on March 11, 1944. They are wearing leather jackets and US tanker's helmets. Cartridge boxes and linked ammo are on the glacis. *National Archives*

The crew members of an M10 with a duckbill counterweight, 803th Tank Destroyer Battalion, 2nd Armored Division, pose by their vehicle at a base at Bodmin, Cornwall, England, on April 7, 1944. Poles at the corner of the hull were for supporting camouflage netting. *National Archives*

During the same photo session as in the preceding photograph, the right side of the turret is shown close-up, documenting a new manner of stowing four musette bags and several bedrolls on the side of the turret. Three ready rounds of ammunition are in the turret. *National Archives*

A view of the left rear of an M10 with markings for the 813rd Tank Destroyer Battalion shows a socket for a camouflage-netting pole in the foreground and a socket with a pole in it to the right. Rolls, a 5-gallon liquid container, and a grouser rack are also present. *Jim Gilmore collection*

An M10 of the 701st Tank Destroyer Battalion, 5th Army, drives between a destroyed German scout car, *left*, and a knocked-out US M4 medium tank southwest of Littoria, Italy, on April 15, 1944. The M10 is driving toward the cameraman, turret traversed aft. *National Archives*

An M10 of the French Army's 3e Division d'Infanterie Algérienne fires on German fortifications in Castelforte, Italy, on May 12, 1944. The vehicle was armed with a .30-caliber machine gun in the front right of the turret in addition to the .50-caliber, which has a 200-round "tombstone" ammunition can. *National Archives*

One of the M10s serving with the 3e Division d'Infanterie Algérienne enters an Italian town on May 15, 1944. Over the turret is a canvas-covered top, perhaps to offer some protection from shrapnel. A helmeted head is sticking up through a gap in the top. *National Archives*

Near Cori, Italy, on May 25, 1944, an M10 tank destroyer (*right*), an M5 light tank, and an M4A1 medium tank sit disabled in a minefield that was cleared only after the vehicles struck mines. The M10 has suffered devastation to the front right bogie assembly and the track. *National Archives*

On May 26, 1944, an M10 tank destroyer attached to the 5th Army proceeds along a road leading into Cori, Italy. To the right is a road sign for Cisterna. A white recognition star is faintly visible between the stowed 5-gallon liquid containers on the glacis. *National Archives*

A T2 tank retriever, based on the M3 medium tank, of Company B, 1st Ordnance Battalion, is recovering a knocked-out M10 tank destroyer near Cisterna, Italy, on May 25, 1944. Dragging from chains to the front of the M10 are the vehicle's tracks. *National Archives*

An M10 of the 8e Régiment de Chasseurs d'Afrique is parked along the road to Frosinone in the Ceccano area of Italy on May 30, 1944. The diamond-shaped component of the regimental flash is visible on the hull. Local camouflage is lightly applied to the vehicle. *National Archives*

In preparation for the invasion of Normandy, US forces conducted landing exercises at Slapton Sands, England, in 1944. This photo of M10 USA number 4082052 "Bonanza," with a deepwater-fording kit, coming ashore is thought to have been taken there. *National Archives*

M10 USA number 4081085 "Bessie" lands at Slapton Sands. A deepwater-fording kit is installed, and five 5-gallon liquid containers are stowed on the side of the hull. A dustcover is fitted over the mantlet, and a folded tarpaulin is lying on top of it. *National Archives*

Part of a tank destroyer battalion assigned to the 5th Army pauses near Valmontone, Italy, on June 2, 1944. Visible are four M10 tank destroyers and several Jeeps towing 37 mm antitank guns. The second M10 from the right has sandbags piled on the glacis. *National Archives*

On June 4, 1944, the date the Allies liberated Rome, a column of US vehicles, including an M10 to the left, enters the city. Multicolored sandbags give extra protection to the thin glacis, bedrolls are lashed to the turret, and a machine gun tripod is over the mantlet. *National Archives*

Even as the Allies were liberating Rome, German forces continued to hold out. Here, an M10 fires on a German position in the suburbs of Rome on June 4. The vehicle has the wedge-shaped turret counterweights. What seems to be a bedroll is on the mantlet. *National Archives*

An M10 Wolverine of the British 20th Anti-Tank Regiment has disembarked on Queen Red Beach, in the Sword Beach area, during the June 6, 1944, landings in Normandy. Above the bridge-classification marking "29" on the final drive are two spare bogie wheels. *Imperial War Museum*

Tommies of the British 3rd Infantry Division receive fire support from an M10 Wolverine of the 20th Anti-Tank Regiment during the breakout from the Normandy beachhead, June 6, 1944. This Wolverine had the late, duckbill-type turret counterweight. *Imperial War Museum*

Several M10s advance to the front west of Saint-Lô, France, on June 24, 1944. The nearest vehicle has sandbags piled on the glacis for extra protection against antitank projectiles. This type of protection sometimes was called "sandbag armor." *National Archives*

An M10 of Company A, 703rd Tank Destroyer Battalion, that has been held in reserve near St. Jean-de-Daye, Normandy, has been called to support troops of the 30th Infantry Division on July 11, 1944. The name "ACCENT" and the code "A 21" are on the hull. *National Archives*

An M10 of Company B, 703rd Tank Destroyer Battalion, makes its way down a narrow lane in a town near St. Fromond in Normandy, on July 7, 1944. The crew exhibits a mix of smiles, fatigue, and wariness. A spool of wire with a hand crank is on a bracket mounted on the right fender. T48 rubber-block chevron tracks are installed. *National Archives*

On July 20, 1944, an American M10 tank destroyer duels with a German position on the outskirts of St. Lô, France. A large recognition star inside a circle is painted on the rear trunk of a deepwater-fording kit. Ample stowed bedrolls and equipment are in evidence. *National Archives*

In Normandy in late July 1944, captured German troops pass an M10 that has the rear trunk of its deepwater-fording kit in place. The turret counterweight is the duckbill type. Rolls of camouflage netting are piled on the rear; tree branches are employed as camouflage. *National Archives*

Five smiling GIs, most likely comprising the crew of this vehicle, peek out from a dugout they have fashioned under a parked M10 tank destroyer in France on July 26, 1944. A reel of communications wire is lying on top of the left headlight brush guard. *National Archives*

Meanwhile, on the other side of the world, M10s of the 632nd Tank Destroyer Battalion, 32nd Division, patrol a beach at Aitape, New Guinea, on July 31, 1944. Several have what seem to be .30-caliber machine guns mounted on the upper fronts of the turrets. *National Archives*

A British M10 tank destroyer advances on a road to Vassy, France, on August 4, 1944. The tank destroyer is heavily camouflaged with netting and local foliage. Such measures were advisable considering the weakness of the vehicle's armored protection. *Imperial War Museum*

On August 15, 1944, Allied forces launched Operation Dragoon, the invasion of southern France. Here, an M10 with a full deepwater-fording kit has come ashore on one of the invasion beaches on D-day. A length of spare track is fastened to the glacis. *National Archives*

An M10 tank destroyer is firing on a German tank across a river in Orléans, France, on August 17, 1944. Sandbag armor is visible on the glacis of the vehicle, and the pile of rubble to the front of it would have afforded some measure of protection to the hull. *National Archives*

"Doughs," as tank destroyer crewmen often referred to US infantrymen, ride on M10s of the 645th Tank Destroyer Battalion through the countryside north of Salerne, France, on August 18, 1944. The troops were with the 45th Infantry Division, 7th Army. *National Archives*

The statue of a French soldier on the World War I memorial at Lonlay l'Abbaye, France, seems to be beckoning to the crew of an advancing M10 tank destroyer on August 16, 1944. Combat Command A, 2nd Armored Division, had taken the town two days earlier. *National Archives*

Two crewmen of a Royal Artillery M10 Wolverine inspect the spindle of the idler wheel in Normandy on August 12, 1944. The track has been removed at the rear to allow removal of the idler, and the track at the front has spooled out from the drive sprockets. *Imperial War Museum*

A pair of British 8th Army M10 Wolverines are parked in the Via Andrea del Sarto in Florence, Italy, on August 13, 1944. The one to the rear exhibits a duckbill turret counterweight. The 8th Army completed the capture of Florence several days later. *Imperial War Museum*

An M10 of the British 72nd Anti-Tank Regiment, 6th Armoured Division, conducts an indirect-fire mission on August 12, 1944. The gun had an elevation of only 30 degrees, so the vehicle has been driven onto an earthen incline to achieve the desired elevation. *Imperial War Museum*

Probably at the same place and time as in the preceding photograph, M10 Wolverines of A Troop, 111th Battery, 72nd Anti-Tank Regiment, 6th Armoured Division, conduct a fire-support mission in the Arno valley near Florence around August 12, 1944. *Imperial War Museum*

A dusty Wolverine assigned to the 93rd Anti-Tank Regiment accompanies infantrymen of the 5th Sherwood Foresters in the vicinity of Petriane, Italy, during operations against the Gothic Line, August 28, 1944. The vehicle is heavily laden with boxes and baggage. *Imperial War Museum*

A US Army M10 tank destroyer rolls past a the wreckage of a destroyed German truck convoy in a town in the vicinity of Montelimar, France, August 1944. Several stowage racks welded from thin metal rods are on the glacis; one of them holds a fuel can. *National Archives*

During an advance on Domfront, France, on August 16, 1944, to the left is the rear of an M10 with a duckbill turret counterweight. The M4 medium tank at the center, assigned to the 743rd Tank Battalion, was about to pace the lead element of the advance. *National Archives*

Under a sign recently hung by the French Underground, the American crew of an M10 tank destroyer are performing guard duty in the center of the town of Dreux, France, on August 17, 1944. A name, unfortunately illegible, is painted on the 3-inch gun barrel. *National Archives*

M10s assigned to the 601st Tank Destroyer Battalion of the 7th Army cross the Durance River during a mission supporting partisans south of Mirabeau, France, on August 20, 1944. The number "31" is marked on the turret counterweights of the nearest M10. *National Archives*

GIs of the 11th Infantry Regiment, 5th Infantry Division, follow an M10 of the 818th Tank Destroyer Battalion into smoke from burning German armor near Fontainebleau, France, on the advance to Paris on August 23, 1944. Two GIs are riding on the rear deck. *National Archives*

M10s of the 701st Tank Destroyer Battalion, 1st Armored Division, are preparing to start a fire-support mission against German positions across the Arno River in Italy on August 25, 1944. A tied-back radio antenna is on the right side of the glacis of the first M10. *National Archives*

Some of the 443 M10 tank destroyers consigned to the French under the terms of Lend-Lease are being unloaded from a transport ship to landing craft for shuttling ashore. All of the M10s visible in the photo have been fitted with deepwater-fording kits. The one being hoisted at the top has six 5-gallon liquid containers stowed on the side of the hull and a spare bogie wheel above the right headlight guard. The M10 to the rear on the landing craft has a raised cover over the turret. *National Archives*

Local citizens gather around a knocked-out M10 tank destroyer of the Seventh Army in the outskirts of Hyeres, France. The left fender has been ripped off and is hanging below the bottom corner of the glacis. Striped aiming posts are stowed on top of the mantlet. *National Archives*

North of Fontainbleau, France, on August 23, 1944, an M10 tank destroyer of the 818th Tank Destroyer Battalion is firing on retreating German forces across the Seine River. This fighting helped lay the groundwork for the capture of Paris two days later. *National Archives*

Two Achilles tank destroyers, turrets traversed to the rear, are crossing a repaired bridge upon entering the village of Pont-Authou, in Normandy, on August 26, 1944. Much equipment is piled up or secured to the turrets and engine decks, and camouflage netting has been applied to the turrets and 17-pounder gun barrels. A German jerry can is hanging from the rear of the closer vehicle.

A US Army M10 rolls over a pontoon bridge over the Seine River near Mantes, France, on August 28, 1944. In addition to the .50-caliber machine gun to the rear of the turret, there is a .50-caliber machine gun to the right front of the turret for extra firepower. *US Army Engineer School History Office*

Another M10 tank destroyer crosses the pontoon bridge over the Seine River near Mantes, France, on August 28, 1944. On this vehicle, a .30-caliber machine gun has been installed on a pintle mount at the front right corner of the opening at the top of the turret. *US Army Engineer School History Office*

701st Tank Destroyer Battalion M10s ford the Arno River in the Cascina area in Italy on September 1, 1944. The site evidently was secure, since all turrets are traversed to the rear. A .30-caliber machine gun is in front of the closest turret but the .50-caliber is dismounted. *National Archives*

A lone M10 tank destroyer is positioned alongside the Leaning Tower of Pisa sometime after the liberation of the city of Pisa, Italy, in early September 1944. Prominent on the turret of the dust-caked vehicle is a white recognition star within a circle. The turret counterweight is the duckbill type. During the American advance on Pisa, the Germans had used the tower as an artillery observation post, and US forces had issued orders, fortunately not implemented, to destroy it. *National Archives*

An M10 is serving as a battle taxi for GIs of the 3rd Battalion, 22nd Infantry Regiment, near Mabompré, Belgium, on September 8, 1944. The soldier at the rear of the hull is standing on the battered exhaust-adapter pan of the deepwater-fording exhaust trunk. *Jim Gilmore collection*

On September 12, 1944, an M10 with hedgerow cutters and racks of fuel cans on the rear deck crosses a creek along the German-Belgian border near Hemmeres, Germany, while another M10 approaches in the background. In the distance is a destroyed railroad bridge. *National Archives*

As American forces rapidly move east after the breakout from Normandy, an M10 tank destroyer crosses a pontoon bridge over the Moselle River in eastern France on September 12, 1944. The fenders are removed and sandbag protection has been added. *US Army Ordnance Museum*

On September 14, 1944, the crews of two US M10 tank destroyers engage the enemy along the German border. On the glacis of the nearer vehicle are stowed two spare bogie wheels, a tool box, and several crates. Bedrolls are lashed to the side of the turret. *National Archives*

An M10 tank destroyer assigned to the 7th Army is firmly mired in deep mud in a field near Éloyes, France, on September 23, 1944. Tarpaulins have been thrown over the hatches and the turret to keep out the rain until the vehicle can be recovered. *National Archives*

It's not clear exactly how this M10 met its fate as photographed in France on September 27, 1944, but it may have rolled over into an antitank trench or natural gully. The resonance chambers and attached exhaust ports are visible below the hull overhang. *National Archives*

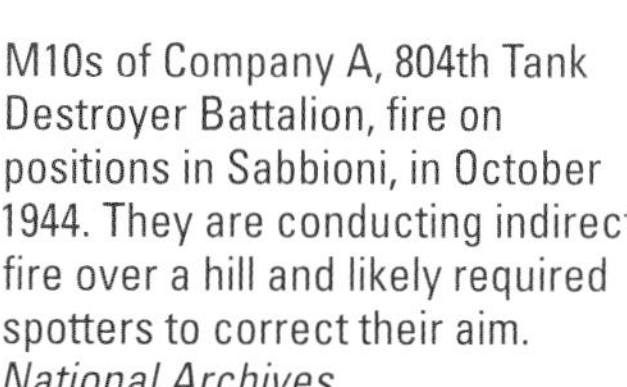

M10s of Company A, 804th Tank Destroyer Battalion, fire on positions in Sabbioni, in October 1944. They are conducting indirect fire over a hill and likely required spotters to correct their aim. *National Archives*

Crewmen of an Achilles 17-pounder from A Troop, 75th Antitank Regiment, British 11th Armoured Division, are performing maintenance on their vehicle during a lull in the action in the Netherlands on October 4, 1944. On the bow are two racks for storing spare track sections. Two wireless antennas are installed: a short one on the recessed mount on the sponson, and a long one on the mount to the front of the assistant driver's hatch.

Once again called on to operate as mechanized artillery, M10s of Company A, 634th Tank Destroyer Battalion, prepare to fire on German observation posts in Aachen, Germany, on October 14, 1944. Crewmen in the background are intently scanning for targets. *Jim Gilmore collection*

During the hard-fought battle for Aachen, an M10 of the 634th Tank Destroyer Battalion fires on a German observation post in the tower at the far end of the street on October 15, 1944. Most of the battalion's efforts that day were focused on enemy strongpoints. *National Archives*

A 634th Tank Destroyer Battalion M10 has just fired on a German position in Aachen on October 15, 1944. The helmeted head of the gunner is just visible above the top of the turret; to his rear is the .50-caliber machine gun, which could be useful in the street fighting. *National Archives*

During the October 1944 Battle of Aachen, US Army troops and vehicles are gathered along a railroad embankment. To the left is an M10 with wedge-shaped counterweights and markings for the 634th Tank Destroyer Battalion. To the far right is another M10. *National Archives*

In a photograph taken at the same place and moments apart from the image at left, an M10 with duckbill counterweights and markings for the 634th Tank Destroyer Battalion has moved up on the left. To the far right is another M10. A D7 bulldozer clears rubble. *National Archives*

An M10 of the 634th Tank Destroyer Battalion blasts away at a German position during the bitter street fighting in Aachen in October 1944. In the background is the rear of another M10. Both vehicles had the wedge-shaped counterweights on the turrets. *National Archives*

Displaced families are huddled against a cliff and next to an M10 assigned to the 5th Army in the war-torn village of Livergnano, Italy, on October 19, 1944. In small letters on the forward end of the hull is the nickname "HITLER'S NIGHTMARE." *National Archives*

The commander of an M4 medium tank to the right keeps watch as an M10 tank destroyer in the distance advances cautiously down a street in Aachen on October 20, 1944. A pile of spent casings by the M10 attest to the fact that it has been busy. *National Archives*

Members of the 818th Tank Destroyer Battalion perform maintenance on their M10s at a site in France on October 29, 1944. On the M10 in the foreground, two GIs wrestle into place a drum marked "D," presumably for diesel, used for the GM 6046 engine. *National Archives*

An M10 of the 645th Tank Destroyer Battalion has taken position in the Vosges Mountains outside St. Benoit, France, on October 31, 1944. A raised structure has been added atop the turret, and sandbags are piled on it. In the turret is Sgt. Robert E. Bailey. *National Archives*

An Achilles 17-pounder is crossing a Churchill Ark bridging vehicle, part of a temporary passageway over the Savio River in northern Italy on October 24, 1944. Tree branches are distributed on the vehicle for camouflage purposes. *Imperial War Museum*

From a position more to the left than that of the preceding photo, an Achilles 17-pounder is driving over the Churchill Ark while crossing the Savio River on October 24, 1944. On the left mudguard is the Viking-ship symbol of British V Corps. Sitting in the river in the background is a German Panther tank with the main gun missing. *Imperial War Museum*

On November 4, 1944, during the long slogging match known as the Battle of the Hürtgen Forest, two M10s of Company C, 893rd Tank Destroyer Battalion, advance toward Schmidt, Germany, in response to reports of a German panzer force in that town. *National Archives*

An M10 tank destroyer has paused during the advance through the bombed-out village of Fresnes, France, on November 9, 1944. Faintly visible on the two parts of the turret counterweight is the black panther symbol of the Tank Destroyer Force. *National Archives*

A 711th Tank Destroyer Battalion M10, "DUKE OF PADUKA," apparently named for the popular comedian called the Duke of Paducah, passes through Metzervisse, Germany, on November 17, 1944. Over the turret is a raised steel cover with a hinged front panel. *Patton Museum*

At an ordnance maintenance shop in Leghorn, Italy, M10s are lined up undergoing servicing, repairs, and perhaps modifications. The one to the right of center has wedge counterweights, while the one to the left of center has the early-type counterweights. *Patton Museum*

Among the vehicles in an ordnance shop are four closely related vehicles: *left to right*, an M36 tank destroyer, an M10 tank destroyer, and two very dirty M4 medium tanks. The M36 with its powerful 90 mm gun first entered combat in Europe in October 1944. *Patton Museum*

US 5th Army M10s place massed fire on German positions along Highway 64 near Bologna, Italy, on November 17, 1944. At least five M10s are visible in the photograph, with more possibly located out of view downslope in the background. *National Archives*

M10 tank destroyers with camouflage netting erected over them on poles are configured for conducting an indirect-fire support mission. They are using the road embankment to angle the vehicles so as to achieve the necessary elevation for the 3-inch guns. *US Army Ordnance Museum*

M10s of the 1/11 Anti-Tank Regiment, 6th South African Armoured Division, fire on German positions along Highway 64 outside Bologna, Italy, on November 17, 1944. Painted on the turret counterweight of the closest M10 is the name "VAGABOND." *National Archives*

At an unidentified locale, possibly in continental Europe in the fall of 1944, two M10 tank destroyers accompany a column of US infantry troops. Each vehicle has two 5-gallon liquid containers stowed on its glacis and the lead vehicle appears to have an extra machine gun. *Patton Museum*

An M10 advances near Zweifall, Germany, at the beginning of a new US offensive against the Siegfried Line on November 15, 1944. A number of riders are on the rear deck, and sandbag armor is arrayed on the glacis. Grousers are on the side of the hull. *National Archives*

Two M10 tank destroyers negotiate a twisting dirt road in the Hürtgen Forest on November 18, 1944. Evergreen boughs are affixed to both vehicles for camouflage, and both of the M10s have a .30-caliber machine gun in the front of the turret opening. *National Archives*

Several M10s roll through a town in eastern France on November 20, 1944. On the closer vehicle, the driver is in the head-out-of-hatch position, usually the preferred mode of driving when the vehicle wasn't in an active combat zone, since his visibility was much better than when buttoned up with the hatch closed. The cows and a French woman under a blanket in the left foreground were killed in an artillery barrage. *National Archives*

This M10 of the 2e Division Blindée (2nd French Armored Division) was knocked out during street fighting in the Battle of Strasbourg, France. The explosion and fire that engulfed the vehicle burned the rubber off the tracks, leaving piles of gray ash. *National Archives*

The crew of an M10 guards a road running through Grosshau, Germany, on December 1, 1944. The building in the background smolders from an explosion of a mortar round. Evergreen boughs have been stuck in the grousers and on the bow for camouflage. *National Archives*

During an advance in the Oberhofen area of France on December 8, 1944, an M10 with the 813th Tank Destroyer Battalion approaches under enemy fire a gap in a log barricade erected by German forces. To the front of the turret is a .30-caliber machine gun. *National Archives*

Soldiers of the 3rd Battalion, 157th Infantry Regiment, attached to the Seventh Army, take cover near a supporting M10 tank destroyer with a duckbill counterweight during a German barrage in Niederbronn-les-Bains, Alsace, France, on December 10, 1944. *National Archives*

An M10 tank destroyer of the 645th Tank Destroyer Battalion negotiates a narrow gap in a German-built log-and-rock barricade in Lembach, France, on December 14, 1944. To breach obstructions of this strength, often it was necessary to employ a bulldozer. *National Archives*

It is not clear where or when this photo was taken, but it is characteristic of the conditions M10s encountered in villages as they fought their way through Europe from the fall of 1944 to the end of the war. Mesh for holding foliage is on the hull and turret. *National Archives*

An M10 of the 654th Tank Destroyer Battalion is positioned to sweep a wide angle of approach at a street corner in Habkirchen, Germany, on December 15, 1944. The barrel of a Browning .30-caliber machine gun is visible above the right front top of the turret. *National Archives*

The crews of a South African M10 unit replenish their ammunition and clean the guns after a fire mission in the Monte Sole area of Italy on December 18, 1944. The vehicles were emplaced on prepared positions on the hillside in a manner to make them level. *National Archives*

An M31 tank recovery vehicle is being employed in an attempt to pull an M10 tank destroyer from a crater in a street in Gey, Germany, on December 16, 1944. The M31 was based on the M3 medium tank. The nickname "DEAD END KIDS" is painted on the M31. *National Archives*

On December 8, 1944, an M10 tank destroyer assigned to the 77th Infantry Division makes its way past ruined huts in Ormoc, Philippine Islands. Very little stowed gear is present on the exterior of the vehicle. To the left is a 75 mm howitzer motor carriage M8. *National Archives*

An M10 of the 632nd Tank Destroyer Battalion is undergoing maintenance at Ormoc, Leyte, Philippine Islands, on December 16. The man on the turret watches a Japanese barge burning. The exhaust-trunk adapter of the deepwater-fording kit is present. *National Archives*

An M10 assigned to B Company, 645th Tank Destroyer Battalion, and commanded by Lt. Fred A. Merritt is prepared to shell German positions in a town in the French Alps. The tank destroyer gained a small degree of camouflage with the scattered snow on the vehicle and the white sheeting on the turret. The two men visible in the turret are wearing fur-trimmed parkas. *National Archives*

A GI inspects an M10 tank destroyer knocked out by the enemy in Mittelwihr, Alsace, France, on December 26, 1944. Two shells penetrated the thin glacis. The headlights and brush guards were mangled. The resulting fire melted the rubber off the right track.

In this undated photo from an unidentified locale in northwestern Europe in the winter of 1944–45, the lingering presence of hedgerow cutters marks these M10s as likely veterans of the Normandy Campaign. The nearest M10 has a thin, hard top held above the turret. *Patton Museum*

In the winter of 1944–45, M10s in continental Europe often were camouflaged with white paint or a whitewash of lime, salt, and water to blend in with snowy terrain. This example has received a white camouflage on most upper surfaces, but not on the running gear. *Patton Museum*

Somewhere in Italy in the winter 1944–45, the crew members of an M10 tank destroyer bear the cold while they await their next target or assignment. The recognition star and circle were applied a bit carelessly, since the star tilts noticeably with reference to the top of the turret. *Patton Museum*

The body of Lt. Col. George B. Randolph lies next to one of two M10s parked along the route of advance of the 90th Division on January 9, 1945. The commander of the 712th Tank Battalion, Randolph was killed in action while leading his battalion into battle. *National Archives*

An M10 crewman of the 636th Tank Destroyer Battalion scans the distance for signs of the enemy near Bischwiller, Alsace, on January 28, 1945. To his front are the perforated barrel of a Browning .30-caliber machine gun and an ammunition box for that gun. *National Archives*

The following series of three photos documents ⅝-inch roof armor installed on an M10 of the 813th Tank Destroyer Battalion in France on January 15, 1945. Here, the armor is viewed from the right front, showing two vision slots in the frontal plate. *National Archives*

The roof armor is observed from the upper front. The top consisted of a fixed forward plate, two front-hinged plates that could be opened, and a fixed, triangular-shaped rear plate. The armor was designed to protect against grenades, shrapnel, and snipers. *National Archives*

The roof armor is seen from the left side. There was a fixed vertical plate with a vision slot to the front, an open space to the rear of it, and a small, fixed piece to the rear. Below the triangular rear roof plate were two fixed vertical plates with vision slots. *National Archives*

The crew of a whitewashed M10 of the 773rd Tank Destroyer Battalion takes a break during operations near Benonchamps, Belgium, on January 21, 1945. A few weeks earlier during the Battle of the Bulge, the crew of this M10 had knocked out five German tanks. *Jim Gilmore collection*

Members of an M10 crew of Company C, 629th Tank Destroyer Battalion, share a campfire with members of the 331st Infantry Regiment in the area of Courtil, Belgium, on January 20, 1945. M10 crews often formed strong bonds with the infantry they supported. *National Archives*

In the middle of a beautiful winter backdrop that belies their deadly mission, two M10 tank destroyers of Company A, 645th Tank Destroyer Battalion, deliver a nighttime artillery barrage on German positions around Sparsbach, France, on January 26, 1945. *National Archives*

A white-camouflaged M10 attached to the 634th Tank Destroyer Battalion performs overwatch duties at the Belgian village of Büllingen on January 30, 1945. Next to it is a US M2 half-track that the Germans captured when they overran the town weeks earlier. *National Archives*

A dead German soldier in a reversible parka, camouflage pants, and *Stahlhelm* lies in the foreground across the street from a building where an M10 tank destroyer and several jeeps are parked. The M10 is whitewashed except on the lower hull and running gear. *National Archives*

An Achilles of the 154 Bde, 51st Highland Division, follows a Churchill flail (*foreground*) on the outskirts of Bruk on February 8, 1945. Typical of armored fighting vehicles of all nations, the outside of the Achilles is covered in gear. *Imperial War Museum*

The village of Rohrwiller, Alsace, France, had been ravaged by recent fighting when this M10 rolled through it on February 4, 1945. A section of track is secured to the glacis, and a .30-caliber machine gun barrel and ammunition box are in the front left of the turret. *National Archives*

A column of vehicles from the 15th Scottish Division, including two Achilles tank destroyers, are assembling at the start line of an attack on German forces southeast of Nijmegen, the Netherlands, on February 2, 1945. Most of the crew's equipment is piled on the roof of the turret and covered with a tarpaulin; bedrolls are secured to the side of the turret. On the sponson to the front of the recognition star is a rack for a driver's hood and windshield assembly. *Imperial War Museum*

An M10 tank destroyer in the background passes a recently knocked-out M4A3 (76 mm) medium tank in Oberhoffen, France, on February 3, 1945. Medics between the two vehicles are preparing to remove the remains of a soldier who was killed in the battle. *National Archives*

Two members of Company I, 313th Infantry Regiment, one with a handie-talkie, are perched on an M10, watching for German movements across the Moder River in Haguenau, France, in February 1945. The turret is equipped with the ⅝-inch roof-armor kit. *National Archives*

An M10 attached to the Third Army fires on an enemy pillbox across the Sauer River near Echternach, Belgium, on February 7, 1945. On the rear deck are racks made of welded strips of metal for holding liquid containers, bedrolls, crates, and other gear. *National Archives*

As the US Army continued to press forward into the German western frontier in February 1945, the US 5th Army continued its drive into northern Italy. Here, during an advance by the 92nd Infantry Division on February 8, an M10 of the 701st Tank Destroyer Battalion passes the ruins of a church in Querceta. A bridge classification number, "30," is on the upper center of the final-drive assembly. Racks made of thin rods are on the glacis for the liquid containers and on the side of the hull. *National Archives*

Vehicles of the French 1st Army pass in review during a parade in Colmar, Alsace, France, celebrating the defeat of the Germans in the Colmar Pocket. In the foreground, driving abreast are two M10 tank destroyers, followed by a number of armored cars. *National Archives*

An M10 provides fire support during an attack on German lines on Monte Belvedere in the North Apennine Mountains of Italy in late February 1945. The vehicle has had areas of white paint applied over the Olive Drab base color to provide some snow camouflage. *National Archives*

An M10 tank destroyer conducts a fire mission against German positions in the Monte Belvedere area of Italy on February 20, 1945. A crude wooden ladder is leaning against the vehicle, and the sticks on the ground were for keeping ammunition stocks dry. *National Archives*

Two members of the 126th Engineers, 10th Mountain Division, sweep for mines after the M10 just beyond them was disabled by a Teller mine near Monte della Torraccia, Italy, on February 22, 1945. The M10 was assigned to the 701st Tank Destroyer Battalion. *National Archives*

PFC Frank Say of the 202nd Infantry Regiment observes for artillery fire from the turret of an M10 tank destroyer firing on a German position near Blain, France, on February 23, 1945. Planks have been stacked against the vehicle for camouflage. *National Archives*

M10s supporting the 8th Infantry Division enter the German city of Düren on February 24, 1945. On the front of the lead M10 is a hedgerow cutter, above which are two bogie wheels with a track-return roller between them. Sandbag armor is liberally applied. *National Archives*

In a Roer River Campaign photograph probably related to the preceding one, an M10 of the 801st Tank Destroyer Battalion advances to attack German forces on the outskirts of Jülich, a few miles north of Düren, Germany, on February 24, 1945. *National Archives*

Troops of the 1st Infantry Division stand alongside two M10s as they await orders to move out in Gladbach, Germany, during the advance to the Rhine on March 1, 1945. The nearer M10, and possibly the other one, has a .50-caliber machine gun over the mantlet. *National Archives*

An M10 of the 701st Tank Destroyer Battalion negotiates a narrow mountain road in the Monte Terminale area of Italy on March 3, 1945, during the advance to the Po River valley. Below to the left, a Bailey bridge is under construction by Army engineers. *National Archives*

Members of the 10th Mountain Division take cover behind a 5th Army M10 tank destroyer in the Castel d'Aiano area on March 3, 1945. German snipers were active ahead, and the M10 offered them some protection and a change to get some much-needed rest. *National Archives*

M10s of a 1st US Army tank destroyer battalion advance through Neuenhausen, North Rhine–Westphalia, Germany, on March 3, 1945. Faintly visible on the side of the upper hull of the M10 in the foreground is wire mesh for applying foliage for camouflage. *National Archives*

US soldiers have flushed a German soldier, *far right*, from a pillbox as an M10 tank destroyer stands by to the left in Mainz, Germany, on March 22, 1945. This M10 has two machine gun mounts in the front of the turret opening and a .50-caliber in the rear. *National Archives*

Acting Maj. Gen. Colin M. Barber, commander of the 15th Scottish Division, is speaking to the crew of an Achilles 17-pounder outside Goch, Germany, during Operation Veritable, or the Battle of the Reichswald, on February 20, 1945. The tank and crew are identified on the photo as part of the 234th Antitank Battalion. Arrayed on the bow are three US 5-gallon liquid containers, three spare track shoes, and three "duckbill" track end connectors. *Imperial War Museum*

An Achilles 17-pounder is providing support for British airborne forces during landings on the east side of the Rhine River on March 25, 1945. Two of the Horsa gliders that transported airborne troops to the site are in the background. The turret has been modified with a steel cover, with ample vision slots, similar to the covers found on some M36 tank destroyers. *Imperial War Museum*

An Achilles 17-pounder from the 6th Guards Tank Brigade along with several British paratroopers are guarding an intersection in Dorsten, Germany, as Churchill tanks transporting members of the US 17th Airborne Division roll past on March 29, 1945. Wrapped around the barrel of the 17-pounder gun and arranged on parts of the glacis is scrim camouflage netting; a roll of the material is secured to the turret. Duckbill end connectors are on the outer sides of the tracks. *Imperial War Museum*

A tank destroyer assigned to the 1st US Army approaches a log barricade at the edge of Wetzlar, Germany, on March 28, 1945. Tank riders and piled-up baggage have hidden the turret features that would indicate whether this was an M10 or an M36. *National Archives*

At an Army Day exhibition for the public at a base on Oahu in April 1945, an M10 tank destroyer is in the foreground. Next to it is an M18 Hellcat tank destroyer. Also in view are a DUKW with the skin removed, an LVT-4, and a 105 mm howitzer motor carriage M7. *National Archives*

An M10 assigned to the 644th Tank Destroyer Battalion is part of a column advancing near Olpa, Germany, on April 11, 1945. It is fitted with a Richardson-type hedgerow cutter. Sandbags and two solid-spoked bogie wheels are on the glacis. Jim Gilmore *collection*

An M10 supports members of the 1st Infantry Division who are clearing remaining German snipers from the town of Sankt Andreasberg, Germany, on April 15, 1945. The turret has the duckbill-style counterweight with packs hanging from it. *National Archives*

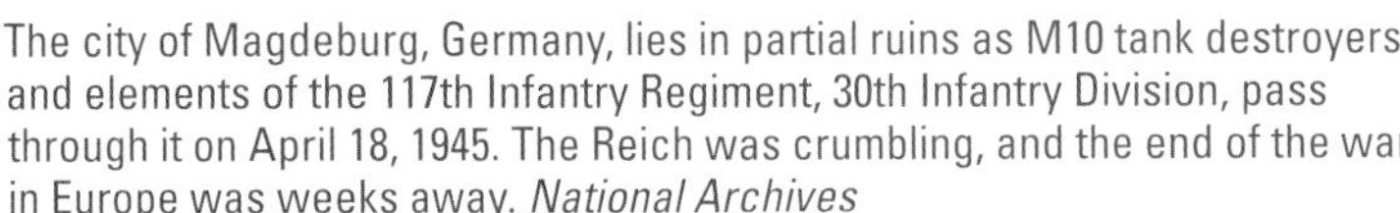

The city of Magdeburg, Germany, lies in partial ruins as M10 tank destroyers and elements of the 117th Infantry Regiment, 30th Infantry Division, pass through it on April 18, 1945. The Reich was crumbling, and the end of the war in Europe was weeks away. *National Archives*

Four members of the crew of an M10 assigned to the 823rd Tank Destroyer Battalion of the 9th US Army pose in the turret for their photograph in a destroyed neighborhood of Magdeburg, Germany, on April 18, 1945. A raised roof is present over the turret. Netting is draped over the glacis, covering what appears to be sandbag armor, since a metal rack, supposedly for holding the sandbags in place, is visible along the upper part of the final-drive assembly. *Patton Museum*

An M10 of the 5th Army is being used as mobile artillery, shelling German positions in northern Italy toward the close of World War II, around the end of the Gothic Line operations or during the spring 1945 offensive. Inside the turret, the loader is grasping a 3-inch round. To his rear is a .50-caliber machine gun, pointing to the left. On the rear of the hull is a makeshift tilted rack, filled with 3-inch ammunition, and more ammunition is piled up on the ground. *Patton Museum*

On April 21, 1945, the final day of the thirteen-day-long battle for Bologna, Italy, a column of the victorious Allied forces, including an M10 in the foreground, clog a road leading into the city. These vehicles appear to be part of either the Polish or British forces engaged. *National Archives*

The crew of an M10 of 1st Platoon, Company A, 701st Tank Destroyer Battalion, scans across Lake Garda, Italy, toward the village of Riva in search of enemy positions and movements on April 30, 1945. Spent 3-inch casings are on the ground to the left. *National Archives*

Infantrymen of the 2nd Lancashire Fusiliers take a breather during the advance to Ferrara, in northern Italy, on April 22, 1945. Operating in support of them were the Achilles tank destroyers parked along the road. Faintly visible on the rear of the sponson to the extreme right is what seems to be the rhinoceros insignia of the British 1st Armoured Division. *Imperial War Museum*

M10s of the 6th South African Armoured Division pass in review before Gen. Mark Clark and other dignitaries at the Autodrome Track in Monza, Italy, in May 1945. That division was attached to the 5th Army from August 1944 to the end of the war. *National Archives*

Two M10s of the 77th Division are prepared to engage targets to their right along a trail near Ormoc, Leyte, Philippine Islands, on December 8, 1944. Both vehicles have adapters for deepwater-fording exhausts trunks. The marking "AT 52" is on the rear of the closer M10. *National Archives*

In October 1944, a new tank destroyer entered combat in Europe: the 90 mm GMC M36. Like the M10, the M36 had a chassis based on the medium tank M4, but the turret was of an entirely different design, with a long bustle that acted as a counterweight and as a compartment for 90 mm ready ammunition. The 90 mm gun was much better suited for combating the heavily armored, late-war German tanks. The differences in the turrets are evident in this photo of an M10, *left,* parked in front of an M36. *National Archives*